RETAILER'S EDGE

Boost Profits Using Shopper Psychology

Bruce D. Sanders, Ph.D.
Consumer Psychologist

Copyright © 2010 Bruce D. Sanders
All rights reserved.

ISBN: 1449941419
ISBN-13: 9781449941413

Contents

1: Can You Read My Mind? 1

2: The Rationally Irrational Customer 17

3: Honor Thy Customer 33

4: It's All About Respect 55

5: The Price Is Right 77

6: Ease Frustrations About Prices 93

7: Make the Total Purchase Bigger 109

8: Change Item & Brand Preferences 133

9: And You, Have You Given Enough Today? 153

Acknowledgements 157

Index 159

1

Can You Read My Mind?

As Caroline is restocking the clothing racks at a Macy's store in Southern California, she sees out of the corner of her eye a woman coming in her direction carrying a Macy's bag. Caroline turns her attention to the customer. There are two things Caroline notices. First, the woman is pulling a dress out of the bag while she continues walking. Second, the woman is biting her lower lip, adding to what seems to be an appearance of nervousness.

"Are you making a return?" Caroline asks.

"Yes. This dress is nice, I guess, but I decided I don't like it."

"All right. I certainly want you to be completely satisfied with purchases you make at our store. I'll get the information I need from you as quickly as I can."

I think that, as a retailer, you'll agree that up to this point and then with Caroline quickly getting the information from the customer, we're seeing a skilled salesperson in action. With her attitude of taking personal responsibility for promptly making things right, Caroline is building in the customer a positive image not only of that one Macy's store in one Southern California city, but of the whole Macy's brand wherever that customer might shop in the future.

But after the mechanics of the merchandise credit are complete, Caroline does something that might surprise you. She says to the customer, "Before you look around our store to select what you'll buy today with your merchandise credit, may I ask you a question?"

"Yes, sure."

"I know you didn't like the dress. I'm wondering if you can think of any of your friends who might find a dress like that to be right for them."

"Oh," says the customer, "I really hadn't thought about that. Well, my friend who was with me when I bought the dress was the reason I got it. She liked it, but said she couldn't find it in her size. When I got it home and tried it on again, I could see it wasn't right for me. Are you saying I should tell my friend the dress is back here? But it wouldn't fit her. She's taller than I am."

"If it's all right with you, I'd like to give you a couple of my business cards. The card has my name and phone number on it. Your friend could come by the store or could call me, and I'll see how we can find her a dress like the one she recommended for you."

Caroline had gone beyond the edge of excellence. In doing that, she was giving her store an edge over the competition. A *retailer's edge*.

∽

Keeping current customers coming back for more is essential to the success of your business, and a good amount of research says it's less expensive to keep a current customer than to win over a new customer. Still, for your retail business to thrive, you must grow your customer base.

Fortunately, it's not either/or. Suppose a current customer tells you how much they like a product or service you've sold them. You might say, "Please be thinking about other people you know who also would like it, and I hope you'll recommend that they come in. May I give you a few of my business cards in case they want to ask for me?" When a happy customer refers you to others, you not only get a new prospect, but the customer making the recommendation builds commitment to you.

Wait, though. What if the current customer *hated* the product or service? Well, your first task is to make it right with a refund or exchange. Next is to discover why it happened. Researchers from University of Michigan and McGill University found that people who dislike a product or service often are surprisingly open to the idea that people they know would love it.

If a customer is dissatisfied because they found the product or service to be defective, it's insulting to ask them to think of who else might want to buy it. On the other hand, if the problem was a matter of taste, it can work to say, "I understand why the product was a bad fit for you. Now that you're more familiar with it, you might know of some people who you think would like it. If you decide it could help them out, I'd very much appreciate your telling them the product is available here."

Giving your retail business this sort of edge does mean going beyond the basics. Yes, the basics are essential to your succeeding. Unfortunately, though, retailers who stay with the basics are too often limited by old habits, superstitions, and hand-me-downs.

Hand-me-downs happen most often in family-run businesses. The adult kids take over the reins, having grown up doing things in certain ways because that's how their parents said things were to be done. Hand-me-downs also happen when inexperienced retailers buy a business.

Superstitions are a driver when the owners/operators try out something, it fails miserably, and the retailer vows never to try it again, not really analyzing why it failed. If you don't try it again, you can't discover if it will work. And old habits are always a driver because retailers are so busy that they find it hard to carve out the time to build new habits.

My objective in this book is to encourage you to explore possibilities for increasing your profitability by moving beyond old habits, superstitions, and hand-me-downs. Because my background is as a consumer and organizational psychologist, my chief tool for meeting my objective is to take what high-quality research says about how retail shoppers really think and behave, blend those findings into my years of experience consulting with retailers, and then share with you specific targeted tactics you can put into action. As Art Freedman and I did in our book *Making Money Is Not Illegal, Immoral or Fattening*, I'll cover lots of tactics and tell you why the tactics work. And to go along with the chock-full-of-hints format, I'll move pretty quickly through the tactics to fit your fast-paced, action-oriented style as a retailer.

Still, all my efforts will be wasted, at least with you, if you don't maintain an open mind in considering what I share with you. More important to you than my wasted time is that unless you give the tactics a try, you'll have gotten little more from reading this book than a break from other ways you're attending to your business. To find full value, adapt the techniques here into what will work for you. Maybe you don't sell women's clothing, you sell hardware. Does it still make sense to say to a customer who is returning an item, "I certainly want you to be completely satisfied with purchases you make at our store. Now I'm wondering if you can think of any of your friends who might find this item to be right for them"? Sure it makes sense. Sometimes. Identify those "sometimes" so you will achieve your retailer's edge.

༄

Retailing thrives on change. The retailer who stands still is, by definition, falling behind. The width and depth of the upset in the economy from the Great Recession of 2008-2009 was something many retailers had never personally experienced before. What was successful in the past should serve as a bedrock for what you do now, but learning just from what worked five years ago in retailing has dangerous limitations. Those are the old habits and maybe the superstitions.

Because I'm certain there will be changes in the environment in which you operate your business and I've seen how each month brings new insights from consumer researchers, you and I also need a way for me to keep you current. My tool for doing this is www.rimtailing.blogspot.com. That's the blog I maintain primarily for readers of this book and for retailers who make use of other services and products from Retail In Motion, LLC, the consulting firm in which I'm a partner. I suggest you bookmark www.rimtailing.blogspot.com as a Favorite, subscribe to feeds from the site, and then check regularly for free updates to all the profit-making strategies and tactics we'll cover together in this book.

An example of an area in which shopper research is regularly adding profit-opportunity truths is sales promotions. Do your sales promotions have legs and do they draw in the right kinds of footsteps? By promotions with legs, I mean those that continue to be effective in generating profitability for you for a while rather than having effectiveness limited just to the time of the promotion. And the right kinds of footsteps are those of shoppers who buy not just the low-margin items you're featuring, but also items which carry *higher* profit margins.

Your best sales promotions will be based on data you've gathered in the past about the shopping habits of your customers. When they buy the type of item you're thinking of promoting with a price cut, what other types of items do they purchase in the same trip? With this information, order those other products in adequate quantities and enough in advance so you're unlikely to run out. Then stock the items in locations in your store where they're easy to find for the person buying a promoted product.

On the other hand, the worst sales promotions lower the perception of item value in the minds of the shoppers. BOGOs—buy one product, get another product for free—carry this risk. Vendors introducing a new item might have you offer the item as a gift when the shopper buys at the regular price another item already attractive to the same target markets. The idea is that the shopper will enjoy the new item so much they'll start purchasing it regularly. This is a wonderful way to build kickoff sales quickly.

RETAILER'S EDGE

But be sure the free product is presented as a sample. In consumer behavior studies conducted at University of California-Berkeley, University of Southern California, Stony Brook University, and Indiana University, researchers found that if a product is offered for free, the shopper becomes less likely to buy the product at full price afterwards. What happens is that when getting it at no charge, consumers conclude—consciously or subconsciously—that the product must be low quality. This is a terrible first impression to leave with the consumer about a new product. It also makes you look bad for giving what appears to be a low-quality gift.

The way to avoid this problem, some of the researchers discovered, was to be blatantly honest with the customer. Tell the shopper in signage, advertising, and salesperson-customer conversation that the free item is being offered as a sample because you believe the shopper will enjoy the product and want to buy it in the future.

That much you can do yourself. But there are two related tactics for which the manufacturer and/or supplier can help: The free product should be clearly labeled as a sample, and it's best if the free item is in a size smaller than any of the standard sizes offered for sale. Also, because developing habits of purchase requires making more than one buy in a row, attach to the free sample a coupon for a customer discount on the next purchase.

⁙

Sales promotions that turn into prolonged price wars are risky. You lower a price as a promotion. Your competitor lowers it further. You respond by meeting the competitor's price and then lowering it even more, at which point the competitor meets your additional reduction, and so on. Your customers can find themselves expecting prices to continue to move downwards. When you can't maintain the drops, your customers' disappointment might cause them to take their footsteps somewhere else.

If you're a major retailer player in your market, one of the tactics to avoid price wars makes use of a principle of social psychology, if not directly of consumer psychology. The principle is "Anticipate how others will respond to what you do." The tactic I have in mind is a "We'll meet their price" assurance. For the smaller retailer, meeting the price opens up the opportunity for a Big Box to drive you out of business by cutting you down. But for the major player, the message to competitors might be, "You won't get any lasting advantage from slashing your prices, since we'll be right there with you." According to an economic analysis posted on the *Time* magazine blog, that message dampens enthusiasm all around for price wars.

Social psychology findings also can be useful in preventing consequences more tragic than price wars: What a dream to have more shoppers rushing into your store than you ever thought possible! But how quickly that dream can turn into a nightmare. Recall how Wal-Mart worker Jdimytai Damour was trampled to death by November 2008 Black Friday shoppers while he was attending the front doors at the Valley Stream, NY store. Recall how in October 2009, customers at a Burlington Coat Factory store in Columbus, Ohio looted and destroyed merchandise when they learned that a woman's offer to pay for their purchases was a hoax.

Understand the psychology of crowds as part of preparing for having people fill your aisles when you hold Black Friday sales, limited quantity sales, celebrity appearances, releases of new video games, and similar events.

- If shoppers will be waiting in line to enter the store or department, have store staff wearing name tags talk to the shoppers. Invite those in line to fill out a sweepstakes form with their name and other identifying information. Because they lose some of their individual identity, and therefore their sense of individual responsibility, people in crowds are driven to actions they would not take otherwise. Name-to-name contact can head this off.

- Distribute the special items throughout the shopping area. Your objective is to scatter out any crowding. When people are in crowds *that they'd prefer to avoid,* they get more likely to panic and to strike out in violent ways.

There are other actions you might think would work well, but could backfire:

- Should you have uniformed security guards? Some people in crowds become less anxious and more responsible when they see staff in police-style uniforms. However, other people—particularly those who consider themselves to be disenfranchised by society—get agitated and angry. If you do use uniformed guards, aim for an adequate representation among them of people who have an appearance like that of the customers.

- Should you extend the hours of the event? Maybe, but within limits. Extend them too much and you lose the excitement which drives buying.

Sometimes the measures I suggest to retailers are based on shopper psychology research, but the reason the tactics turn out to be successful could be due to something else or, more likely, a combination of factors.

Let's say you run a toy department in a store in North Carolina. Your order of toys arrived. The distributor gave you an excellent purchase price, great store displays, and even videos to train staff on selling the toys. You ordered these toys because you'd learned customers are buying them well in other market areas, and you're the first in your area to carry them. You expect to see high sales profits.

Then today as your employees were stocking the first group of the toys onto the store shelves, you saw a featured Google News story saying a dangerous defect has been found in some toys from this manufacturer. When you take your daily tour of the sales floor, you notice that each time a child picks up a box to look it over, an adult with that child tells the child they can't get the toy because of the manufacturer.

You go back to your office and when you do your own checking, you find that none of the toy product lines you're selling has been found to contain defective items. There is every reason to believe these toys are perfectly safe. Knowing this, what can you do to improve sales of those toys?

Plenty. For one thing, you could remove all the toys in that product line from your shelves, store them for a month or two until memories about the product recall fade, and then return the toys to your shelves. Another possibility is to use signage and personal selling to let customers know you are aware of the recall and to inform them that the toys you are selling were not included in that recall.

And then there's a method that might not occur to you. It's an unusual method that will work only if you have ample shelf space, but consumer psychology research suggests it could work well in helping you to sell your stock and avoid storage costs: Space out the boxes containing the products. University of Utah research findings suggest that when a product is feared to have a defect, putting the boxes further apart leads shoppers to think the one they purchase is less likely to have the defect.

You keep the stock sparse, never fully facing the shelves with toys from that manufacturer, and sure enough, weekly tallies show that sales of the toys have picked up steadily. But is this really due to the "spread out the bad news products" effect suggested by the University of Utah research findings? Unless the defect is a communicable disease, the spacing of the boxes should have absolutely nothing to do with product quality. To think otherwise is superstition. As you realize by now, I've no special place in my heart for retailers who operate by superstition. Yet there are times we'll find it better to work with the superstitions of our *shoppers* than to try to talk them out of the superstitions.

In any case, maybe the true reason sales climbed steadily from week to week is that, as time went by, shoppers forgot about the news of the dangerous defect. Or maybe parents correctly reasoned that all the bad items had already been recalled. Maybe shoppers saw that the shelves with other toys were fully faced, so they figured the toys from this manufacturer must be in especially high demand. They decided to load one or two or three into the shopping cart before all of those supposedly popular toys were gone.

Hey, whatever the reason or combination of reasons, spacing out the products worked to boost sales. Should you really care why? My answer is that you should care. This is why high-quality consumer psychology research findings are such a good basis for the tactics. Research helps us discover not just *what* is happening, but *why* it is happening. But again, on your end, you must use a skeptical eye. Before putting time and money into adapting and then implementing a tactic, see if it makes sense to you as a professional retailer that the adaptation will work.

༄

Because you're a professional retailer, the payoffs you see in the tactic might be much more than what the psychological research suggested. Let's go back to the case of Caroline and the return of the dress. To help Caroline's customer think about who might end up being interested in a dress like that, we'll want Caroline to ask the customer why she's returning the dress. Asking for reasons has more to it than that, though:

The annual Return Fraud Survey conducted by the National Retail Federation usually finds that the most common reason for fraudulent returns is a person wanting money or credit for what turns out to be stolen merchandise. In the 2009 survey, about 43% of the retailers said that people are using counterfeit receipts. So add another procedure: When someone comes to the returns counter, ask them to tell you the reasons for the return, and then record those reasons along with the person's identification information. Never make this procedure a prolonged inquisition, and always have in mind that it is more important to keep a customer than to keep to a policy.

Still, your request should be more than the formality of checking a box for the category of reason. It should be a brief interview. As word gets around that you do this, the dishonest consumers become more likely to decide to take their business elsewhere. And that's fine with you, since their business consists of fraud.

Okay, there's still some consumer psychology to it. The key to doing this well is to prove to your honest customers that they'll enjoy benefits from telling you the reasons for their merchandise returns. Your staff might say something like, "I know it's a bother to you to have to return merchandise you've bought here. We want to be sure we deal with suppliers who will provide you, your family, and your friends with reliable products the first time, every time." Then do regularly summarize the reasons and make merchandising adjustments based on what you discover.

∽

All of this is not to say every profit-making tactic sparkles like gold at first glance. Some work because they give you a subtle edge over the old, conventional retailing practices used by your competitors. Consider the New York University finding that sales of indulgence products tend to climb if the products are featured in places adjacent to products that shoppers believe they *should* purchase. It might take a little thought to recognize how we believe we've earned the right to indulgence after we've bought—or as it turns out, even considered buying—a virtue product.

What's best is that all the little and big tactics you implement as you read this book add up to creating a store personality. Among other things, this can influence how successfully you ride out problems. Like this one:

An item you intend to sell for $1,699.99 has some digits missing from the Internet price. It's being offered for $9.99. What a deal for the customer! What a headache for you!

This is what happened to electronics retailer Best Buy at the end of summer 2009. What happened next is a case study about apologizing for sour lemonade mistakes.

- Orders flooded in over the Internet. Store shoppers lined up, many clutching a printout of the online ad.

- Best Buy promptly shut down order-taking for the item, posting a statement saying, "We sincerely apologize for this error and make every effort to ensure issues like this do not happen.... While we are truly embarrassed that this occurred, Best Buy will not be able to honor the $9.99 price."

- Some of the purchasers who'd already gotten their order confirmations now turned their flood from sweet to sour, filling online forums with bitter complaints and threatening legal action.

- Then the sweetness came from a different source. Posts appeared on those forums reading, for example, "Yeah, someone screwed up, but Best Buy carries a lot of customer good will going into this. They usually have the best prices and treat customers well." Even a fellow who started a website to protest Best Buy's withdrawal of the $9.99 offer ended up writing, "... they have received a HUGE amount of publicity over this matter. Now, they seem to be the only ones walking around with a smile on there [sic] face knowing that they have received completely FREE advertising."

Research findings from Stanford University would suggest that Best Buy came out of this looking so good because the stores have what is labeled as an "exciting" more than a "sincere" brand personality. Retail stores come to have a personality in the minds of customers and prospective customers. Some businesses are seen as daring and spirited, while others are seen as cautious and intellectual. It works best when you decide what personality you'd like your store or website to have and then carefully design advertising, merchandising, signage, staffing, and all the rest to strongly project that personality.

Here are five dimensions consumers use in understanding your store personality:

- Sincere or witty. In what ways are you honest? Wholesome? Cheerful? Teasing?

- Exciting or predictable. To what degree are you daring? Spirited? Imaginative? Trendy? Responsible? Dependable? Persistent?

- Expert or inquisitive. In what ways are you knowledgeable? Successful? Calm? Confident? Secure? Imaginative? Curious?

- Sophisticated or approachable. To what degree are you formal? Assertive? Ambitious? Casual? Sociable?

- Rugged or luxurious. In what ways are you gruff? Challenging? Indulgent? Cooperative? Trusting? Considerate?

By carving out a clear store personality, you make it more likely customers and prospective customers will think about your store, and that in turn can lead to additional business. Fit your store's retailing personality to how your target market members want to see themselves. But realize that whatever you choose to be on each of the dimensions will always carry some good and bad points. For instance, stores with a sincere, predictable, or expert personality are usually highly respected, but may have trouble keeping customers after a product recall, bad customer service, or the sort of thing Best Buy had to deal with. That's because the target market members don't like surprises when the surprises make it look like the retailer is inept.

On the other hand, with stores that have a witty, exciting, or inquisitive personality, customers are ready for a reaction like, "We make shopping more fun because we offer the unexpected," and, "We're always learning so we can get better and better."

Which mix of these five dimensions will distinguish your retail business in ways that are most profitable? What will you be doing *today* to start projecting that mix? What is the personality of your retail business, and what are the best ways for you to turn sour lemons into sweet lemonade when the inevitable mistakes happen?

RIMinders

- When a customer returns quality merchandise that didn't fit their needs, consider asking the customer to refer someone who might like the item.

- Avoid BOGO—buy one product, get another product for free—sales promotions, since they lower the perceived value of the product.

- Calm crowds in your store by relating to shoppers by name and spacing out in the shopping area the high-demand items.

- With any good-quality products which have been associated with bad news, stock the products on shelves in ways that provide plenty of space between items or packages.

- Use advertising, merchandising, signage, and staff-customer interactions to project a clear store personality.

2

The Rationally Irrational Customer

If you've spent any time in retailing, you've discovered the special advantages of hiring employees who are over 65 years old. They frequently bring with them decades of knowledge and a patient acceptance of the customer rudeness and staff politics which frustrate younger workers. Empty nesters appreciate the chance to get out of the house to be with other people on a regular schedule. Much retail employment is part-time, and for many retirees, part-time work is fine.

But older employees do have their senior moments. With advanced age comes trouble remembering details. Instructions get confused. Names of customers and customer preferences are forgotten. What's a boss to do? Well often, when a senior citizen employee starts showing signs of forgetting, the supervisor cuts back on the physical demands. No more climbing ladders, less walking up and down stairs, fewer requests to go to the receiving dock to fetch restock merchandise.

The trouble is this makes things worse. A research review by psychologists at the Beckman Institute in Illinois says energetic physical activity is one of the best remedies when memory abilities start to fade in older adults. Be overprotective and the abilities of your older employees will deteriorate even more. It also makes other employees angry at the older employees for not pulling their own weight and angry at you, the boss, for letting it happen.

Do you let your senior citizen employees fully use their abilities to help you achieve maximum profitability? When you think it best to protect employees and customers by limiting the duties of an older employee, do you discuss it with the older employee to get their ideas first?

∽

Communication with your older employees will take you far in your journeys to maximum retailing profitability. So will communication with customers. Consider the matter of you being out of stock. Having come through months when predicting shopper demand was so difficult, retailers' caution in ordering is perfectly understandable. Still, frequent out-of-stocks (OOSs) are a major reason customers will stop shopping with you. One risk in being out-of-stock is that you'll miss the opportunity to make the sale. But the longer-term risk is that customers will stop thinking of your store as the place to go for an entire product category, and perhaps other product categories as well.

What counts in all this, of course, is your customers' definition of "out of stock." And here's a payoff from survey research. A survey sponsored by the IHL Group, based in Franklin, Tennessee, found customers often say the store is OOS even when the retailer thinks the store is in-stock. This is because the customer has a broader definition than the retailer does:

- The shelf is empty. Even when you attend to your point-of-sale and inventory level data—as you should be doing frequently—you might miss the fact that items to fill in the empty shelves have not made it from your receiving or storage area onto those shelves.

- The merchandise is on a shelf, but not easily available to the customer. It could be on a high perch, which puts it out of sight, or in a locked cabinet, which puts it out of reach, when there aren't store staff members right there to help.

- The customer is looking for an item with characteristics you're not tracking. They want a specific pattern on the skirt or a smaller quantity in each package. Your recordkeeping systems indicate you have the item, but unless your staff members are talking with the shoppers, you won't realize that, in the customer's view, you're OOS.

With the tough economy, it's especially important that you don't waste money. Among other things, this means cutting back on stocking merchandise that fails to earn you an adequate profit. But ask yourself if carrying that item serves a function other than frequent sales. You might be carrying items with very low turnover—and therefore very low payback by themselves—because stocking these items lets customers know you carry a complete set. The buy-it-once-in-a-lifetime fasteners are on the shelf because your store is known for carrying whatever a customer might happen to need in the way of fasteners. But don't carry more than a couple of each of those slow sellers.

Cut back duplicate merchandise lines. Can you reduce your good-better-best assortment choices to better-best choices? Do you need to have five different bedroom ensembles on display when you could have three on the floor and offer to special order others?

Avoid carrying products that fit into limited categories for the customer. Retailers who stocked products labeled Jell-O Gelatin Flavors for Salads learned that buyers used the products just for salads. In tight economic times for the retailer, it works better to carry boxes labeled Jell-O with serving suggestions that include salads, among others. Over the years, Church & Dwight Co. has done a masterful job of positioning Arm & Hammer Baking Soda in a considerable variety of categories for the consumer, from odor control to cleanser to, well, baking soda.

RETAILER'S EDGE

When you show and tell customers about the multiple uses of items, you lower the chances that they'll see you as being out of stock on something the customer wants. But where do customers get off having their own definitions of out-of-stock in the first place? Those shoppers are so irrational. There is really absolutely no way of even making educated guesses about what will please them! Right?

We've all heard retailers say things like that. Perhaps like you, I find myself thinking those sorts of things even when not saying them aloud. The truth though is that we all—retailers, customers, and I'll even throw in vendors and regulatory agents—are fairly rational. The trouble isn't irrationality. It's that we human beings are so complicated. Our task in retailing is to untangle the complexity and to make rational what strikes us at first as irrational.

One area for this is appreciating how shoppers vacillate between seeking conformity with others and seeking to be different from others. Maybe rules apply to this phenomenon at least sometimes, such as in restaurant orders.

When you dine at a restaurant with friends, do you want to know what everybody else is ordering before deciding what you'll order? Do you do that because you're simply too lazy to look through the menu? Is it because you might want to suggest sharing a dish? Or is it either because you want to be sure you fit in by ordering what others are ordering or be sure to order another selection to demonstrate your independent nature?

When people in a group are all buying and each person's selection is announced in sequence to the others, there are some people who will seek out what's different from what others are selecting. Therefore, it's useful for you to have sufficient variety in your best-selling product types. But other shoppers will want to buy exactly what others in the group are buying, so it's useful for you to have enough stock of those particular items.

Whether a shopper is a variety seeker or conformist depends in part on the degree of conformity of others in the group. Again using the restaurant experience as an example, consider the findings of an observational study conducted with diners at Flam's in Paris by researchers from Sorbonne-Assas in France and University of Adelaide in Australia. The researchers found that when anywhere between about 30% and 80% of a group had ordered the same choice, people placing their orders next tended to go along with ordering this choice for themselves. But once the conformity exceeded 80%, subsequent orders were much more likely to show variety seeking.

If you're selling socks or socket wrenches instead of steaks, and if you're doing business in Paris, Texas, not Paris, France, the percentages will probably be different. But in any case, do your merchandising and selling with the expectation you'll be having both conformists and variety seekers as shoppers.

༄

Changes in our mental sets and the individual differences going with all that are good news for retailers. For example, some people feel like an ESC and some people don't.

Extended service contracts (ESCs) are a profitable add-on sale for you. They also can add to customer satisfaction, since if a product fails to function properly, a good ESC avoids the customer having to exchange or discard the item. But most consumer advocates recommend against ESCs. They say the average cost of an ESC is much higher than the average cost of making necessary repairs to the product. They also say that when customers purchase ESCs, they're telling the store it's okay to carry merchandise that breaks down.

Never leave a customer believing you've encouraged them to make a bad decision, so never pressure your customers into purchasing an extended service contract. But researchers at University of Maryland, Rice University, and Carnegie Mellon University find that there are situations

RETAILER'S EDGE

where an ESC is a worthwhile escape for the purchaser. In these cases, you'll want to describe the advantages.

- Purchasers who operate on a limited budget can find it very difficult to pay for replacing the product if it breaks or in handling any unexpected costs for repairs. They'll appreciate your pointing out to them that, in buying the ESC now, they're making a fixed payment, removing lots of unpredictability.

- Purchasers of pleasure-related technology products, such as video game controllers, don't want to be deprived of use of the item for even a brief time. They're willing to pay for an ESC that offers prompt replacement of the product if the defect can't be fixed immediately.

- Purchasers who are expected to repair every broken product in the home—maybe a husband being viewed this way by his wife—may be happy to pay a fee to avoid the time and trouble of repairing at least this one product.

When you see the opportunity, point out the value added by an extended service contract. If the purchaser has just gotten an unexpectedly low price, the potential for sale of an ESC grows. That's only one of a number of reasons for you to arrange unannounced discounts on items commonly purchased in your store.

At first glance, it might seem to be really bad business to surprise a customer with an especially low price on items the shopper had already intended to buy. After all, they'll buy the items at the price they had expected, so why give up any of the profit? But consumer behavior researchers at University of Arizona, Arizona State University, and University of Pennsylvania found that just such a practice, used with care, can end up building your profits. The reason is that customers who are grateful to you will buy more from you, such as the add-on purchase of the ESC, and nothing brings out gratitude in a customer more than finding a surprisingly low price on an item the customer already had intended to buy.

They'll buy more from you over time, and they'll also spend more than they'd originally planned to spend during the shopping trip where they found the surprise special. The researchers discovered evidence that what's behind the extra purchasing is a desire to reward the merchant. It's not just a matter of getting items at a better price. That's why the shopping cart total goes up.

On top of all this, these shoppers become more likely to tell others about the excitement they experienced when in your store. That makes it more likely you'll have those people coming to you as well. The key to doing this effectively is to maintain the element of surprise. Don't discount most items on the person's shopping list, and don't stop advertising the low prices on those popular items which will draw traffic into your store. But knowing you offer surprise specials will motivate all that traffic to move up and down your store's aisles on a treasure hunt, and what better way than this to make shoppers aware of *all* the products you offer them?

Most everybody loves a bargain, but still there are differences among shoppers. Such as general differences by gender. Psychoanalyst Sigmund Freud claimed that pretty much everything we do springs from the sex drive. Lots of people thought Sigmund was taking a good thing too far. Still, it's true the sex drive does sell. In using that fact to improve your retailing profitability, realize the sex drive refers to more than raw passion. In consumer psychology, it means the mutual attraction of masculinity and femininity toward each other. It's the Yin and the Yang.

RETAILER'S EDGE

In most retailing cultures, consumers associate masculinity with products and services that are disciplined, stable, and serious and associate femininity with products and services that are delicate, whimsical, and changeable. Your customers make purchase decisions based in part on how well the purchase will project their desired degrees of masculinity and femininity.

It's true across age groups: Children as young as twenty months old distinguish toys intended for girls from those intended for boys. Northwestern University research found that boys are much more likely than girls to prefer rough chunky peanut butter to the smooth variety. It's true across cultures. Classic research by a psychologist working for IBM showed how the descriptions of masculinity and femininity might differ from one culture to another, but every culture places high importance on its definitions, whatever they are.

What stays the same is the drive of each type to show off their credentials via product use. Consider cell phones. In America, many men prefer a compact-looking cell phone to project a serious high-tech image. But a *Wall Street Journal* article reported that many Indonesian businessmen had been aiming to achieve their serious look with an old Nokia model nicknamed The Brick because of its heft. Businessmen in both countries were showing off, but in ways influenced by the culture and therefore with implications for your retail merchandising. If you'd stocked your shelves with The Brick in Indonesia, you'd have made big sales. If you'd stocked your shelves with The Brick in America, there's a good chance you'd be left with lots of worthless bric-a-brac.

Get the point? All right then, I've a Yin-Yang quiz question for you: First, here's the situation: Some British researchers noticed a gender difference in where customers keep their cell phones while sitting in a club. Women are much more likely than men to take out their phone from purse or pocket only when they are ready to use the phone. On the other hand, men are much more likely to place their cell phone in a highly visible location soon after sitting down.

The researchers figured that the men were placing their phones on the bar or table because they wanted to show off to others that they possessed the latest and greatest model. But to whom were the men interested in showing it off? The women? The other men? Both?

Here's your question: Which one of these four caused the greatest jump in how often the men would take out their cell phones, put them on the bar or table, and begin toying with them, even when not placing calls?

A. As the number of men in the area increased?
B. As the number of women increased?
C. As the percentage of men compared to women increased?
D. As the percentage of women compared to men increased?

The correct answer? Well, it appeared that the men were preening with their cell phones to disarm the competition in the same way that male peacocks pump up the strutting and feather preening when there are at least a few females around and then a bunch of other males come by. The third choice in my list of four is the correct answer.

What's this all mean for you? If you want to sell your customers—especially your male customers—the latest and greatest, there's an advantage in stocking items with a distinctive design easily recognizable even in a dimly lit club.

Do that, and you'll earn the gratitude of your shoppers. It isn't customer loyalty I'm aiming for coming from that gratitude. It is the creation of *advocates*. Advocates praise you to others. You might think that if you increase the number of advocates by, let's say, ten percent, this would lead at best to about a ten percent increase in sales. In reality, though, according to research reported in *Harvard Business Review*, the effect of creating new advocates is much greater than that.

- You create advocates by maintaining a welcoming shopping environment where your customers love to be.

The result is that advocates spend more time with you, and this makes it more likely they'll buy more products.

- Advocates are people who appreciate you and your staff for meeting their service expectations. Advocates want your business to succeed. If they see something they know they could buy at another store or website for a bit less, they still prefer to give their money to you.

- Advocates want to help you out. They'll tell family and friends, and even shoppers they come across in your store or in competing stores, what a good job you do. If they hear criticisms of your business, they want to reassure themselves they're right in their feelings, so they'll talk down the criticisms.

It's no surprise, then, that when you increase the number of advocates by the ten percent, you can easily realize a much greater increase in sales.

Store advocacy goes beyond customer loyalty. Store advocacy means how often and how strongly your customers praise you to other potential shoppers with specifics. Beyond "I love to shop there" to "I get an excellent price on top-quality herring," "Almost everyone there listens to my questions and gives me useful answers," and maybe most important of all, "I don't go out of my way to recommend stores to people, but I feel very good about recommending this one to you."

The trouble with you stopping at customer loyalty is that retail analysts have been pointing out for some time now how customers aren't all that loyal, even if they ever really were over the past few decades. Current customers may enjoy shopping with you, but with the exception of your family and close friends, unless you work consistently and vigorously to maintain that habit, current customers won't hesitate much in giving their business to somebody else. The term "customer relationship marketing" is excellent shorthand for reminding us retailing professionals of the importance of every transaction between the shopper, on the one hand, and on the other hand, the staff members, the signage, the reward programs, the cleanliness of the parking lot, and on and on.

As researchers from Memorial University of Newfoundland point out, customers don't often describe their interactions with retailers as "relationships." Give your customers lots of specifics to praise you about as they talk to others. Go ahead to ask them to tell others about their experiences in shopping with you. To encourage them to practice doing this, regularly ask your customers how you are doing.

My definition of "word of mouth" is "influential information a source consumer tells a shopper who trusts the source." WOM usually occurs between friends or family, but considering the definition, it could include a trusted salesperson telling a shopper about the salesperson's experiences with a particular product, brand, or store. WOM traditionally happened face-to-face from one person to another. But now it often happens via blogs, social network sites, and review sites. The essential element, though, is trust. The shopper receiving the information trusts the consumer who provides it.

Research says that WOM has a measurable influence on about two-thirds of all consumer goods sales and overall is more influential than media advertising. WOM is particularly powerful when a shopper doesn't know much about the product category. If I want a new exercise machine, but don't know much about exercise machines, I'm open to advice. If I want to dine at a nice restaurant in an unfamiliar city, I welcome leads from gourmets who have lived there for a long time.

Again, the influence of the advice depends on trust. Give your staff and customers ideas for what they can say to others to praise your store and your product mix in ways that the WOM sources are trusted. Perhaps surprisingly, one important key in establishing this trust is that the WOM communication include at least some criticisms or concerns about what's being recommended. If everything's coming up bright lights and lollipops, it sounds phony.

Another key is that the advice include specifics. "When you use this exercise bike, you'll feel like you've had one excellent workout. But I have to say the instructions to use it were a little complicated," is more believable, and therefore more likely to convince the shopper than is, "This is without doubt the best exercise bike I've ever used."

⁓

Whenever I complete an important purchase in your store, I'd like to walk out the door confident I made the right decision. I don't think much about it with the automatic purchases, the ones I make week after week from habit. But especially if it's a big-ticket item or one where I think other people will be judging me, I want to be sure to get it right. I want it so much that I'll put energy into convincing myself and others what a smart shopper I was.

Let's say my purchase decision was a ticket at a horse track betting window. In a classic consumer behavior study done at a race track, the researchers found that *after* somebody bet on a horse, they became even *more* confident the horse would win. If we're uncertain about the bet, we get worried.

Researchers at Arizona State University noticed how powerful this is while themselves participating in an office betting pool about the outcome of the TV show *Survivor*. People predicted that their bets would boost their pleasure in watching the show, since they'd get more involved.

But the outcome was the opposite. Betting made watching the show *less* pleasant.

We don't want our customers leaving our store or our website worried they might have bet wrong. That's why we'll follow up with purchasers by reassuring them with the reasons you think that they made a good decision. Have product literature available to your shoppers to take away with them not only before they complete the purchase, but also afterwards. Attach your business card to the packet. Encourage the customer to show the product literature and business card to their friends and family. Invite them to come back to tell you how the purchase worked out, and when they come back with a happy story, admire their skills in making the right bet.

Then once you build up that advocacy, associate it with the name of your store. Handle the name of your store as a brand which projects just as strong an image as the name appearing on labels on any of the products your store sells. In a shopper survey sponsored by the Wharton School of Business, the Verde Group, and the Retail Council of Canada, the single most important driver of customers coming back was what the researchers called "brand experience."

- How exciting is the design of your store, and how imaginative are the ways you work the name of your store into the décor? Each time the name of your store appears on a shopping bag, do the font, the color, the background design, and the rest all team up to project the personality you want people to notice and remember?

- How consistent is the quality of your products balanced against considerations like price? Plenty of shoppers will sometimes want to pay less and so will settle for "better" instead of "best." But the customer who buys a product they've known to be the best expects to get that same sterling quality when they buy another product with the same name on the label. Whenever your store's name appears as the house brand name, the quality level should be predictable, whether the product is green beans or auto shock absorbers.

- If your store is one of a chain, if you operate under a franchise, or if you're in a retailer cooperative, the name you use is probably used by others. How well are you teaming up with those others to help them project the quality of the brand? When you discover better ways or tools for doing business, are you sharing those ideas with your namesakes? Do you take time to thank them for what you learn from them about upholding the brand name's reputation?

Make it tempting for people to say the name of your business and your business motto or tag line. After all, you do want them talking about you. So I'm thinking about Emigh Ace Hardware in Sacramento, California, a wonderful store named after a store founder who probably had the pronunciation of "Emigh" mangled every which way from Sunday over the years of his life. Above the store entrance and alongside the store name is a picture of a girl in coveralls saying, "Call me Amy." Amy also appears in each ad circular published by the business.

I'm also thinking about the fashion house in the United Kingdom called fcuk. Okay, I'm willing to consider that when Stephen Marks founded the company in 1972, he decided to call the company French Connection United Kingdom and afterwards was absolutely astonished at realizing what the acronym would be and then, later, that the main website URL would be fcuk.com and the American branch would be called "fcuk US," but taking all into consideration concluded that French Connection United Kingdom was such a great company name that he'd have to just put up with fcuk.

I'm willing to consider that, but isn't it more fun—and maybe even more accurate—to consider that the process worked the other way around, with Mr. Marks and his colleagues intentionally choosing an edgy name because they thought target market members would get one tremendous kick out of looking at it, saying it, and telling others about it, just as I'm doing now? This way, more fame would come to the company.

RIMinders

- Collaborate with your older employees to keep them as physically active as their health allows.

- Make sure that any merchandise your shoppers count on you having is kept easily available.

- If you sell extended service contracts, make a special effort to offer the ESCs to purchasers on a limited budget and purchasers of pleasure-related technology products, and point out to all customers the advantages of an ESC for people expected to repair their broken products themselves.

- Give unannounced discounts on items commonly purchased in your store.

- To boost sales of technology products, merchandise those shelves with items that have easily recognizable, distinctive designs.

- To develop advocates for your store, regularly ask customers for specifics on their experiences shopping with you, including ways you can improve.

- When customers complete an important purchase, tell them why they made an excellent decision and have product literature available for them to take with them.

- Choose a business name and motto that people are tempted to say.

3
Honor Thy Customer

This rich business executive brings in a grandfather clock—a treasured family heirloom—to a repair shop because the clock has neither ticks nor tocks. The man behind the counter says, "I estimate the repair cost to be no more than $100. Shall I go ahead?" The executive gives the okay.

Then, without hesitation, the repairman spends just short of three minutes carefully looking over the clock, listening to the clock, and feeling the gears inside the clock. It appears to the customer as if the repairman is even smelling the case.

Suddenly, the repairman folds his left hand into a fist, sharply knocks the left top side of the clock case, hands the clock—now ticking loudly—back to the executive, and says, "That will be $80, sir."

It takes a few seconds for the executive to wipe the smile off his face because he's thrilled the clock is working again. Finally, he musters up a scowl to go along with saying to the repairman, "Where do you get off charging me $80 for simply tapping the side of my clock?"

The repairman nods somewhat wearily, as though he's heard this sort of thing before. He answers, "Oh, for tapping the side of the clock, I'm charging you $5. The other $75 is for knowing where to tap."

Then the repairman remembers reading about a consumer psychology study conducted at University of Singapore and University of Toronto. The researchers found that when service duration is shorter than the customer expected, the customer thinks the service is inferior. So the clock repairman says to the rich business executive, "You didn't need to stand here for a long time waiting for me to fix the clock. You didn't incur the time, expense, and bother it would be if I'd said, 'Leave the clock with me and come back in a week.'"

Now the executive with the clock understood.

If questions come up about your fee for quick services, do you remind your customers how quicker completion of services is better?

Unless you're a massage therapist, of course.

༄

Even the most sophisticated of shoppers can easily forget that for those who have more money than time, time can be more valuable than money. As a retailer, you can gently remind them. On the other hand, sociological research finds that many people with lots of money and little time miss carrying out some of the activities they did in the past, such as gardening and shopping. We might note that the rich executive in the clock story didn't delegate the family heirloom repair errand to somebody else.

Different consumers have different objectives. While taking account of our own constraints on time, money, staffing, and other resources, let us personalize the shopping experience for consumers of all ages.

For instance, with over 400 locations on five continents at last count, Build-A-Bear Workshops stores can be considered testimony to the success of allowing shoppers to personalize what they buy. Each child selects from a range of items in the store to design their own stuffed animal, and upon completion of the toy, the child signs the animal's birth certificate.

People love the opportunity to put their personal imprint on their acquisitions. They buy accessories for their iPods and automobiles. A few years ago, online clothing retailer Lands' End told *Fortune Magazine* that fully 40% of Lands' End shoppers are willing to pay more and tolerate longer delivery times so they can specify a blend of precise sizes when ordering.

Researchers at Colorado State University found that consumers choose to personalize even if it means accepting design quality inferior to what professional designers would produce. Another study concluded that shoppers in a marketing atmosphere filled with fears of privacy being violated still will volunteer ample amounts of information about themselves to a retailer if they see the retailer using this to personalize the shopping experience for them.

Your shoppers appreciate the chance to *customize*. But what they like even more is the opportunity to *personalize*. So present the options to your shoppers in terms of them expressing their personal values. Lands' End talks about the luxury that comes when having clothes cut to produce maximum comfort for the customer.

It's easiest for you to offer personalization when you accept special orders. However, that's not the only alternative, and accepting special orders does bring up complications—such as how to handle merchandise returns—which you might choose to avoid. Offering accessories as add-on purchases is another approach. And in fact, doing no more than having sales staff call customers by name is a bit of personalizing the shopping experience.

When you get to know your store's repeat customers, you can do the best job of personalizing your approach and recognizing how they'd prefer to personalize their purchases. But even the same person will change over time and from one situation to the next. Therefore, let me change what I said a bit ago. A more accurate statement is that different consumers can have different motivations *at different times*. Still, customers are not completely unpredictable. The changes customers make in their expectations are based on some fairly stable individual personality characteristics.

So how do we know what the customer expects? By paying attention to what the customer says and what the customer does. When Caroline noticed that the woman walking toward her in the Macy's store looked nervous while pulling the dress out of the bag, Caroline decided that the woman could use some reassurance about it being okay to return an item. "I certainly want you to be completely satisfied with purchases you make at our store," said Caroline.

In deciding how to personalize the retail sales and service, many consumer behavior experts divide people into groups based on those underlying personality characteristics. One grouping you might find useful comes from fans of psychoanalyst Carl Jung. Dr. Jung said that consumers see a salesperson as playing a role in a shopping drama. People shop to solve problems, and clinical research convinced Jungians we expect specific sorts of problem solvers in our lives. Here are the five big ones, using my adaptations of the language of Jungian theory:

- The Superhero takes responsibility for rescuing us. The customer expects the Superhero to go above and beyond what most salespeople are able or willing to do.

- The Coach reassures us. The customer expects the Coach to be available until the problem is solved and to encourage the customer to get whatever is needed to solve the problem.

- The Guru brings experience and a sharp mind. The customer expects the Guru to know the customer's needs without asking lots of questions.

- The Playmate loves fun. The customer expects the Playmate to be more interested in how the shopping experience *feels* than in how the product or service *works*.

- The Rascal exploits other people. Customers with strong morals don't like being around the Rascal. But there are plenty of shoppers who count on the Rascal to help them solve problems in ways that take advantage of the good will or the naiveté of others.

Jung and his students concluded that people throughout different cultures of the world all use these same five roles in their thinking. This convinces Jungians that each of us arrives in the world with these templates inside our brains. Not only are we born to shop, but we're also born with clear expectations of shopkeepers.

If that's what our customers expect, don't let them down. Prepare your staff to form a team with each shopper by analyzing if the shopper wants a Superhero, Coach, Guru, Playmate, or Rascal today and then responding to those expectations in the shopping drama.

☙

Notice that this Jungian framework puts most shoppers into only one of a set of types and assumes that a shopper won't change types after interacting with the people in your store. This sort of thinking can be useful when a salesperson has to decide instantly how to respond to a customer. But this view of consumer decision making does not do justice to the complexity of the human mind.

During my teenage years, I learned that Robert Benchley was one of my father's favorite writers. Benchley had achieved his greatest fame through his published books and brief articles and by having appeared in a bunch of movie shorts in the 1940's. Chances are that you have at least heard of Robert Benchley's grandson, Peter, who wrote the decidedly non-humorous novel *Jaws* and coauthored the screenplay.

RETAILER'S EDGE

There are loads of delicious Robert Benchley quotes I've come across. The one that comes to mind now regarding the silliness of putting shoppers into just a few categories is, "There are two kinds of people in the world, those who believe there are two kinds of people in the world and those who don't."

A more accurate view of shoppers is that each person is at a certain point on a dimension between extremes, and that interactions with your store staff, your store signage, your product marketing, and more can move the person to a different place on the dimension for better or worse. One important dimension is the frequency with which a customer shops with you. We'd like to move them in the direction of coming again soon and often. Frequent shopper programs can help with this. These are often called "loyalty programs." I suggest thinking of them instead as "frequent shopper programs" because that's a more accurate description of what they do. Customer loyalty is wonderful, but the evidence is that it is often too fragile, shallow, and fleeting.

Whatever we call them, these initiatives reward customers for their continuing business. When well-designed, they motivate the customers to keep coming back in order to obtain the rewards. Overall, the reward most popular with customers is a percentage discount on future purchases of items selected by the customer. Other popular rewards include discounts on items selected by the retailer and a free gift with a purchase.

Customer loyalty programs add to your profitability by increasing sales and by helping you target your sales promotions. At the time of enrollment, you can gather information like the person's address, family size, and self-expressed objectives in shopping with you. Then you can track each participant's shopping frequency and what items are purchased. The low costs of database management make it realistic for almost any retailer to collect and analyze the information. But survey research finds that prospective enrollees do want to be convinced their privacy will be protected.

One selling point for shoppers which is often overlooked by retailers is the sense of prestige that participation gives. According to frequent shopper program researchers at University of Pennsylvania and University of Southern California, people like to be recognized for store loyalty. Based on those research findings, here are some tips for getting the most from frequent shopper programs. Be able to answer "Yes" to these questions:

- Do the enrollment materials, the enrollment procedures, and the participant card all clearly refer to the customer as a "member"?

- Do you have multistep programs, in which a member can move from green to gold status, for example, by increasing the total amount and/or the frequency of purchases?

- When the customer shows the card to the cashier at the time of checkout, does the cashier give extra acknowledgement, such as by looking at the customer, smiling, and saying, "Thanks for being a green step member"?

- Do you tailor the program to the customer's culture?

Customers with a Western mindset tend to prefer programs in which rewards come incrementally. For each dollar or euro you spend, you get points. Smaller rewards are available for a small number of points and larger rewards are available to those who save up their points. Be sure the redemption rules are easy to understand. Then each time the customer makes a purchase, print the current point tally on the receipt. Minimize the surprises.

On the other hand, customers with an Asian mindset tend to prefer frequent shopper programs which offer larger rewards earned with an element of deserved fate. Give sweepstakes entries or lottery tickets. Name the program with words that signify good luck.

Because many Asian cultures stress duty to the group over individual glory, avoid publicizing the identities of big winners. Otherwise, those big winners and all those who see the publicity may come to fear that the program tempts fate in ways which could bring bad fortune. In fact, it can be even more important to the Asian consumer than to the Western consumer that they know they earned the reward. Researchers from Baruch College, University of California-Berkeley, and San Francisco State University surprised people with promotional gifts of appreciation. Those from the United States enjoyed their surprise gifts more than did those from Hong Kong, Singapore, Taiwan, or Vietnam. Because the reward appeared to be unearned, the East Asian recipients seemed to feel it produced a menacing imbalance.

Keep in mind that a major objective of a frequent shopper program is for you to maintain up-to-date information about your customers, including what they purchase and how to contact them with marketing materials. That can become harder to do when your customers are paying more attention to price than to other elements in the value equation, such as helpful sales staff or customer-friendly return policies. Those program participants start shopping at another store, and you get out of touch with them.

Even if you're the price leader overall, another store might be offering a highly discounted special on selected items, so the shopper who is feeling short on cash will go there for those items. For these customers, the frequent shopper program loses momentum, since they don't see themselves progressing on the road to the payoff.

Research findings from University of Southern California and University of Pennsylvania provide a tactic for addressing the problem: Maintain customers' interest in their loyalty program participation by giving them credits for coming to your store, even when they don't make a purchase. In fact, this method is also effective in convincing new shoppers to sign up for the loyalty program.

There are two key points to making it work, though:

- What you want to produce is a feeling of regular progress on the road to the loyalty program reward while building the habit in the shopper of keeping your store in mind. Therefore, you might offer a bonus stamp or credit once each week for the shopper just coming into your store.

- Customers tend to assess their progress in terms of percentage of completion more than in terms of the dollar value of the bonus or number of bonus points. Therefore, build the momentum by keeping participants aware of how close they are to the next reward benchmark.

Giving away frequent shopper credits might strike you as bad business. However, Iowa State University research found that shoppers accelerate their purchasing as they see themselves getting closer to earning a reward. That's the payback.

༶

Expertise forms a dimension that affects how soon and how often shoppers return. At one extreme of the dimension are the customers who think the retailer has much more expertise than the customer does. At the other end of the dimension are the customers who believe they know all they need to know and, if anything, want to show off their expertise to the store staff.

To help me explain how all this can help your profitability, may I make a three-part request of you? First, please think of a product category you carry in your store that has technical specifications. Maybe a television? Batting practice machine? Parquet flooring? Weed killer?

Second, imagine that the Three Musketeers stroll into your store looking to buy an item in that category. They're all dressed in modern clothes and they left their swords back at the condo, so they don't draw much special attention from the other customers. The thing is the three of them don't come into your store together. First, Anthos arrives. It turns out he knows very little about the product category. An hour after Anthos leaves, Aramis arrives. He knows a moderate amount about the category. And one hour after Aramis' departure, Porthos bounds by. He's not only an expert in the product category, but is considered to be an opinion leader.

That brings me to the last part of my request of you: Please guess which musketeer is likely to ask the most questions of salespeople about the technical specifications for that product category you carry. Will it be Anthos the Novice, Porthos the Expert, or Aramis the In-Between?

Look up from the book for a moment and decide.

Is this your final answer? Maybe your thinking was already along the lines of what repeated findings in consumer behavior research say about this sort of situation: People who know lots about a product category or know only a little about it usually ask fewer questions than the shoppers who know a moderate amount.

People with little knowledge say they couldn't think of questions to ask. And those with lots of knowledge? One reason they limit their inquiries is that they believe they already know all they need to know. Another reason is that they are afraid of looking to anybody who is with them as less than experts. The correct answer to my question is that, of the Three Musketeers, Aramis the In-Between is the one most likely to ask lots of questions.

But the lesson here might have more to do with Porthos the Expert than with Aramis. Experts buy the upgrades. They're profit centers. Coach your sales staff to project respect whenever a shopper flashes their expertise. Make it easy for the expert. Let's team up with them, never embarrass them by directly challenging their self-proclaimed knowledge.

This doesn't mean at all that we should draw back when asked for advice. It means that even if finding ourselves playing the Jungian role of Guru, expertise will often be better received by the customer if the advice is given with a bit of uncertainty. In a *Journal of Consumer Research* article wonderfully titled "Believe Me, I Have No Idea What I'm Talking About," a group from Stanford University reported that expert restaurant reviewers are more influential when the reviewers say they're less than completely certain about their conclusions.

Based on that finding, here's the hint for retail salespeople who are seen as product or service experts by shoppers: Avoid coming across to the customer as absolutely certain in the recommendations you're making. The bit of uncertainty makes the customer more comfortable in asking questions and expressing concerns.

Those questions and concerns are highly valuable to you when facilitating the sale. You can present counterarguments or you can steer the customer to an alternative which will better fit their needs. On top of all that, a tone of certainty risks leaving the customer with the mistaken feeling that whatever they do or don't do with the product they buy, everything will work out perfectly.

Still, that's not the whole story from the Stanford study: In three different experiments, the researchers gave study participants a well-written restaurant review identified as coming from either an expert or a novice critic. In some of the reviews of each type, the authors had an attitude of certainty, while in the other reviews, the tone was of some uncertainty. Again, the participants who read reviews by somewhat uncertain experts were more influenced by what was said than when the tone was of certainty. But the findings were reversed when the reviewer was identified as a novice. Here, the reviewer's uncertainty hurt credibility instead of helping.

Why? In my opinion, it's because the combination of "novice" and "uncertain" led the consumers to downplay what the restaurant critic said. If your customers will see your salespeople as novices, it might help for your salespeople to avoid coming across as at all uncertain. But a much better alternative is for your salespeople to learn their trade so well they're consistently seen by your customers as experts.

Among the most profitable ways for you to use Facebook, LinkedIn, Twitter, blogs, themed message boards, and other Web 2.0 tools is to share your expertise and that of your store's staff. Contribute valuable advice to potential customers. When readers recognize the value, they'll build trust in your expertise and gratitude toward your business. *Advertising Age/ARC* survey findings indicate that trustworthiness is among the most important determinants of which retailer a consumer selects. And gratitude opens up the consumer to award you their business.

For your advice to end up being seen as valuable, it must be both accurate and actionable. Regarding accuracy, notice how much bogus information appears on social networking sites. Many observers lament how gullible we all must be. They point to how readily many of us accepted in late 2009 that six-year-old "Balloon Boy" Falcon Heene could be airlifted long distances in what a *New York Times* op-ed piece later called a "supersized Jiffy Pop bag." And a *Newsweek* article complains about former television personality Suzanne Somers, with no formal medical or scientific training, spreading wild ideas about preventing and curing cancer. But it is this supposed gullibility which provides the opportunity for you, the retailer, to use social networking to your advantage. You can spot what you know to be nonsense. Then you can post a correction right there, being sure you sign it in a way that lets readers contact your store or website.

That brings us to the second point: Give *actionable* advice, not just criticisms of what's been posted. If you sell products or services actually shown to help head off cancer, tell the world what to do. Findings from consumer psychology research at Cleveland State University and Case Western Reserve University suggest that social networking users are most likely to put your advice into action when you reflect on the stories of others, refine what's already been posted, and explore alternatives.

⁓

Let's imagine you're a consumer who is wanting to play better golf. You've just walked into a sporting goods store to buy golf balls. As you make your way to the proper department, what a thrill it is for you to spot a little indoor putting green right there. You pick up a club and hit the ball. It goes right into the cup. You try again, and again make it in with only one putt. Now ten more tries. For eight of them, the ball goes right in.

The evidence is now clear. You are one highly skilled golfer. When the salesperson comes over, you ask to see the professional quality balls. They cost much more than the others, but with your abilities, you don't want to waste money on toys.

Hey, wait a minute. Before you make the purchase, you should know about the accomplishments of Katherine A. Burson. No, she's not a professional golfer. She's an assistant professor of marketing at University of Michigan Stephen M. Ross School of Business. A while back, Prof. Burson and her colleagues invited participants to putt golf balls as part of a research project. For some of the participants, the cup was ten feet away. For the others, it was three feet away. No surprise that those putting the shorter distance sank more shots. But the reason I think you should know about Prof. Burson before buying your golf balls is that she found that those putting the shorter distance also were much more likely than the others to think they were skilled golfers and then say they'd be willing to purchase high quality, high priced golf balls. Probably needlessly.

In another study, Prof. Burson and her colleagues administered a quiz about photography to a group of participants. For half the group, randomly selected, their quiz consisted of eight simple questions. They were bound to get high scores. The quiz for the other participants consisted of eight tricky questions. They were sure to get failing scores. After completing the quiz, all the participants were asked about their preferences for each of a set of digital cameras.

Yes, you know where we're going with this. Those who took the tough quiz tended to favor lower-tier cameras, and those given the easy quiz favored more advanced cameras.

Prof. Burson's research findings indicate that in general, your shoppers are not as accurate as they think they are in assessing their levels of expertise. A bunch of other research finds that in the absence of objective evidence, we tend to think we're more talented in a variety of areas than we really are. The problem that comes from this is that both your shoppers and you are exposed to additional risk. The risks for shoppers range from wasted money up to things like serious physical injuries. The risks to your business come from customers who are dissatisfied and perhaps angry about the poor fit between their needs and the product or service they purchased.

The fit improves when your customers have what is called a "consumption vocabulary." Let's say you operate a wine shop. A customer you don't recall having seen before inquires if you carry a wine he had recently tried at a restaurant and truly enjoyed. The trouble is he can't remember the name of the wine. You ask him to describe what it tasted like. Your thought is that if you don't carry that particular wine, you can find something with parallel characteristics.

Unfortunately, the man shakes his head side to side and says, "I'll know it when I taste it." You can't open every bottle. If only this shopper had a vocabulary to describe wine tastes. Dry. Sweet. Smooth. Pungent. Big. With such a vocabulary, you might not need to turn your question from

"Can you describe the wine?" into "Can you describe the wine bottle label?"

Consumer researchers talk about helping customers develop a consumption vocabulary so they can better describe to the salesperson what they're looking for. This can speed up the purchase of the item. The more promptly you can recognize the customer's desires, the happier that customer will be, and happy customers are more likely to shop with you again.

Research finds that shoppers with consumption vocabularies don't spend less time in the store on average. They spend more time and they end up buying more items than the customer who lacks the vocabulary. This is because the vocabulary allows the shopper to appreciate the differences among products. To someone without the words, it all tastes the same.

If you're that wine shop operator, you could run some wine tasting events to teach a consumption vocabulary. Whatever line of merchandise your store carries, develop vocabularies that will make the shopping experience richer for the customer and the sale richer for you.

Consumption vocabularies in customers are especially useful for a retailer who is finding it best or necessary to operate in crowded conditions. It might be because you're forced to move to a smaller store, but you're wanting to present customers the same product mix within that less spacious footprint. It might be because you were able to make a great buy on merchandise from a retailer or vendor who has had money problems, but now you need to decide how much of the new merchandise you can fit on your current shelves. Or the selling in more cramped quarters might be because your traffic flow has increased substantially as other retailers have gone out of business.

When you find yourself conducting retail sales in tight quarters, you might be tempted to cut back on the breadth and width of your product selection. That *could* be your best alternative. However, before doing this, please note the findings from researchers at Columbia University and University of British Columbia: On average, when shoppers from Western cultures are in tight spaces, they want greater variety among products. If they have fewer choices, they'll become less comfortable. Uncomfortable shoppers leave the store sooner and resist returning to shop with you again.

So what to do? The answer comes from another research study, this one done at University of Pennsylvania. Shoppers who initially see a limited variety in the breadth and width of merchandise become much happier, and therefore stay around longer to shop, when the retail store helps them develop a consumption vocabulary to recognize the differences among the products. The shoppers don't feel so trapped by limitations on their freedom to choose. In signage and in customer-salesperson conversations, you'll want to categorize products because customers seek categories. But especially in the more cramped store, also highlight the differences among the product offerings.

Developing a consumption vocabulary works both ways. The customers are also teaching us the words they already use in thinking about selecting, purchasing, using, and even disposing of products. We want to move the customer to a point on the expertise dimension where we give the customer the opportunity for this kind of exchange of information. That is, in case the customer wants this. Sometimes the customer wants to come into the store, grab an item, and be on their way. They've come to your store because they know you carry what they want. In the customer's estimation for that shopping trip, the compelling evidence of your expertise is that you've managed to stay reliably in stock. That's all for this day.

Still, even when the customer is in a hurry, opening up an exchange of information can give you added power in influencing what the shopper buys. I'll tell you why I say that. Are you ready for a surprise?

Most salespeople see it as their role to give out information about the merchandise, not to ask the customer for opinions about the merchandise. But researchers at the Hong Kong University of Science and Technology found that asking a customer their opinion is a powerful selling technique. To use this tactic, you need to understand something a bit strange about how it works: When a shopper is asked to select which of a small group of products the shopper prefers, the shopper gets more likely to want to buy the *next* product considered. The effect is strongest when a shopper is in a hurry to buy a number of different items.

This technique can be of special value in making add-on sales. The salesperson asks, "What do you think of these different items you've looked at?," and then after listening to the answer, "What other items may I help you find today?" The cashier at the checkout counter asks, "What do you think of the items you found here today?," and then after listening, at least briefly, to the answer, suggests an add-on item for the customer to look at next time they are in the store.

The traditional meaning of the phrase "Ask for the sale" is, "After you've presented all the information, don't forget to finish by asking the customer to make a purchase before they wander away." Now an additional meaning is to make the sale by asking customers for their opinions.

In asking customers for their opinions, you're building their self-esteem. That can be a contribution to your community, and I'm a great fan of retailers contributing to their communities. Especially to the community of young people, who are your future customers.

For most retailers, children are an influence market, giving suggestions to the adults on what to purchase. The chief evidence can be seen in the cereal aisle at any grocery store. But according to a *Wall Street Journal* article, about one-third of parents say their kids also actively participate in deciding which automobile the parents should buy.

For all retailers, children are a future market, with their high potential to remain or become primary customers in five to fifteen years. Because of children's roles as a future market, you've a responsibility to the wellbeing of your business and your community to cultivate kids into good consumers. University of Minnesota research indicates that a prime time for doing this is when children are ages seven to eleven.

Around age seven, children's consumer skills start to blossom. Over the next few years, they become much better at recognizing the *benefits made possible* by product features, moving beyond a focus on the product features themselves. Their understanding increases for the correlation between money and value. They gain a greater ability to compare products and to do it on more than one dimension—such as ease of use and duration of use—at the same time. They get better at realizing that more is not always better, such as a strong sour taste being well-suited to pickles but not to peanut butter.

Here are a few tips on developing consumer skills in the seven- to eleven-year-old:

- First, take your lead from the reactions of the parents. When the kids were younger, the shopping mall Santa Claus was smart enough not to promise the kids anything the parents hadn't signaled was a guarantee. Now that the kids are older, continue in the spirit of Santa Claus. If the parents look uncomfortable, draw back from educating the young consumer.

- Second, take your lead from the reactions of the child. With a younger or smaller child, it often builds rapport to crouch down when talking with the child. However, if the child looks uncomfortable when you do this, stand right back up. In any case, never touch the child except perhaps to shake hands if that's culturally appropriate.

- When discussing purchase choices with the parents, also look at the child periodically. If the child asks questions, answer in terms the child can understand and with no hint of ridicule. What seems obvious to an adult might be puzzling to a blooming consumer.

- With the limited time you have available when making a sale, put the top priority on talking to the family about the *benefits* from product features instead of only about the product features.

- Give the family adequate privacy to make their purchase decisions. This is especially important with low income families. One of the most difficult tasks for these families is denying their children what the children want. The families that do it well succeed by privately explaining their financial situation to the children.

Attending to purchasing habits of seven- to eleven-year-olds isn't only to build profits for the far future, though. For some product categories you carry, kids might be a less-than-obvious primary market right now. Consider cell phones. For parents, the target appeal is they won't let the tracks of their kids, when they're away, go cold. On the other hand, for the kids, having the right cell phone is way cool.

Perhaps this is even more true for both parents and their offspring as the children grow into teens, which brings to my mind the name John Vasconcellos. John was a highly popular California State assemblyman from 1967 to 1997—becoming chairman of the influential Assembly Ways and Means Committee—and then a California State senator for eight years, not running for reelection in each case only because of term limits.

To those outside California, John Vasconcellos might be best known as the founder of the California Task Force to Promote Self Esteem and Personal and Social Responsibility. John, a firm advocate of positive psychology, pushed forward legislation to fund programs based on the idea that raising teenagers' good feelings about themselves would make them behave more responsibly.

John did insist that since taxpayer money was being spent, the programs should be rigorously evaluated. It turned out that teenage gang leaders whose self-esteem was raised did not, in fact, change their criminal behaviors much. Yes, they kept up the stealing, beatings, and revenge killings. So what *did* change? It's that the teenage gang leaders felt better about themselves while engaging in all the criminal behaviors. John's self-esteem promotion and John himself were roundly ridiculed. California government funding for the programs ended.

As far as I know, evaluators of the Vasconcellos-sponsored California programs never looked at the relationships between increasing teenagers' self-esteem and their retail buying habits. This mantle was assumed more recently by some Illinois and Minnesota researchers who discovered that when teenagers are praised for their legitimate accomplishments, those teenagers become less likely to make foolish retail purchases.

Retailers who come to know their teenage customers and then learn about their academic, sports, and other large and small victories can help create repeat shoppers for the long term by giving justified praise. The teens are bound to blush and stammer when praised, but they'll buy more wisely. Their families, and eventually the teens themselves, will end up appreciating you for that.

To move each customer, regardless of age, to the sweet spot on the dimension of exchange of expertise, know when to talk and when to stay silent to listen and learn.

RIMinders

- While taking account of our own constraints on time, money, staffing, and other resources, let us personalize the shopping experience for our customers.

- In using frequent shopper reward programs, refer to the participants as "members" and give a small reward to members for just coming in to shop at your store, even if they make no purchase.

- Help customers develop vocabularies they can use to describe to you what they want and to appreciate the meaningful differences among the products and services you sell.

- Figure out what each customer is really asking for—and decide how you will respond to those expectations.

- In order to do a great job delivering what a valued customer wants, pay attention to what the customer says and what the customer does.

- Respect your customers' expertise and praise them for it. Offer your own expertise with a bit of uncertainty.

- Help children and teens become more sophisticated, more confident consumers.

4
It's All About Respect

Selling to a customer often requires you to change a negative attitude into a positive one. It's easier to change an attitude when you know what purpose the attitude is serving for the customer. According to research from University of Michigan, customers are asking themselves at least one of the following questions when their attitude influences their purchases:

- "How easily can I make this purchase decision?" If the shopper has had bad experiences with a brand of product, then the shopper keeping a negative attitude about everything carrying that brand name makes decisions quicker. If you—the retailer—want to change the attitude, make it easy for the customer to consider this particular item to be an exception to their rule. Say, "This product is superior to others carrying that brand name," when this is the case.

- "How well does this item express the values I pride myself on having and showing?" If the customer asks where an item was produced, maybe they place special importance on buying what's produced by American taxpayers, on avoiding items that might be manufactured under exploitive conditions, on protecting their children from agricultural chemicals, or on something else that comes from the customer's values. You could ask the customer, "What's important to you when considering a product like this?"

- "What more do I want to know about this item before I let myself get comfortable with it?" Some negative attitudes arise when the customer isn't sure what to do in an unfamiliar situation. Ask, "What questions may I answer for you about this product?." It also can be useful to take away some of the pressure, while not letting the customer leave altogether, by saying, "I suggest I help you find some of the other items you're shopping for here today, and then we can come back to considering this one."

Almost everybody loves to take a chance at least occasionally. But when it comes to shopping decisions, consumer psychology researchers find that everybody wants to avoid excessive amounts of six particular types of risk. Here are those six categories along with ideas to get you thinking about how you can respect the wishes of your customers—and prospective customers—to avoid unwanted risks:

- Functional risk. "Will the product or service solve my problem or meet my needs effectively and efficiently?" Have at least one sign in your store announcing that product performance is guaranteed.

- Financial risk. "Am I paying too much money?" Know what your competition is charging. If you are charging more, be sure the customer is told what you offer that the competition doesn't.

- Time risk. "If I make this purchase, does it mean investing too much time for what I gain?" See to it that your products and services are easy to use, unless you sense the shopper wants complexity for prestige.

- Social risk. "If the people I admire will discover I'm using this product or service, am I in danger of falling out of favor with them?" Encourage shoppers to bring along friends and family on shopping trips and to contact them via cell phone from inside your store.

- Psychological risk. "Does using this product or service conflict with the image I want to maintain of myself?" In personal selling, learn the shopper's values so the purchase benefits which you present are compatible with those values. In self-service shopping, use ads and displays to communicate a range of purchase benefits so the shopper can find at least one that resonates with their values.

- Physical risk. "Is my health or safety or that of those I love in danger if I use this product or service?" Provide expiration dates, safety instructions, and recall notices for all products where those are available and appropriate. Help protect your customers from making dangerous decisions.

Here's the sort of thing I mean by protecting your customers: After an unusually windy storm blew by my home, left behind was a huge limb from a liquid amber tree blocking half the street. Tree debris much larger than that limb was down all over the area, so it would take a while for city crews to reach my place to slice up and haul away the limb. Since it was obstructing the view of an area where neighborhood children often cross the road, I decided to cut up the limb myself and pull the pieces out of the way.

I figured that the bigger the chain saw, the quicker I'd get the job done. With that in mind, I asked the guy at the equipment rental shop for the biggest chain saw around. As it happens, he asked me absolutely no questions in return, except which credit card I wanted to use. What I dragged back to my car was a chain saw really much too powerful and cumbersome for me to use, given my limited experience both with chain saws and with playing defensive end on a National Football League team.

The danger to my personal safety became clear as soon as I started up the chain saw. I realized that I needed to stop the saw, drain out the gas and oil, pack the saw back into my car, and drive to the shop to make an exchange. As I say, I needed to do all that. But I didn't. Instead, I managed to hack up the tree limb while leaving my own limbs intact. How fortunate for the equipment rental shop, since a customer without fingers has trouble pulling out credit cards.

I wonder if the operator of the equipment rental shop knows about the customer disservice created at the front desk with me and many others each day. I didn't ask him or her, but I'll ask you: How well do your staff protect their customers from making dangerous decisions?

∽

Never overlook the value of a good scare. Yes, it's true that coming across to your customers as the villain from a horror movie might succeed only in scaring off the sale. But consider this: Life insurance sales professionals regularly bring up to prospects the rather frightening possibility that the prospects could die at any time.

What are two lessons we can learn from the successful life insurance sales tactics to apply to our retail selling, whatever the product or service?

- People usually avoid what they should prepare for. As a Californian, I can bear witness to how well many people ignore the possibilities of major earthquakes, for instance. When we as retailing professionals make customers aware of the true risks facing them, we are doing a service.

- Raise the fear because you've a product or service to offer that will substantially reduce the worry. Unless the customers come to believe that you've a remedy, many will ignore the risk in order to make the fear go away. But those customers who won't or can't ignore the risk will stay afraid and probably just get quite irritated at you for arousing the fear. Either way, you've lost a sale. Many consultants advise retailers to arouse enough fear to scare people into action, but not so much that they tune out the retailer. In my opinion, a better guideline is to raise enough fear of a real danger to win the customer's attention, but only to the degree that you've a guaranteed way to substantially reduce the risk. Don't oversell.

- And a bonus tip from retailers who sell skydiving lessons: There are customers who are not at all uncomfortable with a sales situation that raises fears. There are people who find that a good scare spices up the total consumer experience.

Beyond a scare, shock might be even better. A few years ago, Volkswagen kicked off a marketing campaign centered on two TV ads designed to shock viewers. In one ad, the TV viewer seems to be inside a Jetta as the driver chats with a passenger. Suddenly, a truck crashes into the car so severely that air bags inflate and the passenger's head is thrust into the airbag. In the other ad, the perspective is again from inside the Jetta as two couples discuss a movie, and again a truck suddenly comes crashing into the car. Viewers see the passengers shaken up, but uninjured. Each ad ends with "Safe Happens" flashing onto the screen.

The impetus for the campaign was the 2006 Jetta's top scores in federal crash tests. The crashes were real, with stunt actors inside the cars. According to Volkswagen, the outcome of the campaign was positive, with the ads causing consumers to get more interested in buying a Jetta.

The ads caused many consumers to do something else, too. Some contacted Volkswagen to ask if any of the actors were actually injured. These people were worried. And some consumers flocked to a website set up by Volkswagen as part of the campaign. On the website, people could recreate or customize their own crashes. These consumers were fascinated.

Those two reactions are quite different. Still, I would not be at all surprised if a number of the people who found out the actors were okay ended up playing the online crash game, and some of those who played the game repeatedly started wondering if the actors came out of the crashes safe and sound.

Shocking ads can pay off. Two tips: First, be sure the cause for the shock is justified. Second, give viewers of the ads ways to feel good after the shock—and that probably means encouraging the viewers to contact you directly.

∽

All sorts of emotions can serve important roles for the consumer, such as when doing salesperson-to-shopper selling of products and services which appeal to tastes and fashions. Talk about the joys the purchase will bring and how sorry a shopper will be if they miss this opportunity to buy. You'll do this because, in general, people make more purchases whenever their emotions kick in.

The boost works best with positive emotions, but activating consumer emotions we think of as less pleasant—such as fear or even anger—can also stimulate purchasing or rental of the right choices. Also, people are more likely to stay highly satisfied about their purchases if they experienced either a burst of joy or a rush of relief at the time of the purchase.

In fact, the overall emotion is often more important than the shopper's objective evaluation of the product's features. Research at University of British Columbia found that a substantial percentage of consumers said they'd chosen an item because they had the right feelings about it, not because the item came out best in any mental accounting of advantages and disadvantages.

In the study, those customers who let themselves be led by their emotions, compared to those who didn't, expressed more satisfaction with their purchase both immediately afterwards and then when the researchers checked back three weeks later. These shoppers would keep their preferences and satisfaction even if they'd been told an article in *Consumer Reports* would have ranked their selection as less desirable than available alternatives.

A lesson from this is that you can both increase your profits and have more satisfied customers when you encourage shoppers to make purchase decisions that feel good to them without requiring prolonged thinking. To accomplish this in ways that maintain levels of risk acceptable to most customers, make it easy to return products and let your shoppers know about that policy.

༄

Customers are more likely to put trust in you when they feel a personal connection. For example, if a customer finds they have the same birthday or place of birth as a salesperson, the customer gets more interested in making a purchase and is more likely to be satisfied with their purchases.

Researchers at University of British Columbia and INSEAD-Singapore set up a study in which a personal trainer offered a fitness program to prospective enrollees. Participants who believed the fitness instructor was born on the same day as them became more likely to rate a sample program highly and to sign up for a membership. And dental patients who believed they were born in the same place as their dentist were more likely to rate their care highly and to schedule future appointments at that clinic.

The influence doesn't operate in the negative, though. That is, if the customer sees that none of your salespeople share their birthday or birthplace, the customer doesn't become *less* likely to make a purchase from your store. Putting all this together, it makes sense for you to let customers know the birthdays and hometowns of your sales staff. Many hospitality retailers already include hometown information on their employees' name badges, and there are retailers who even announce the birthdays of floor employees loudly and proudly in the store.

Discovering commonalities builds a feeling of trust, even when the trust is not necessarily justified. Customers prefer conducting transactions with salespeople who are the same religion, race, or ethnicity as them. But the researchers found that having something in common can take you only so far. If the customer found the salesperson to be rude, the good will evaporated. In highlighting the similarities, also keep it clear that you're cultivating a business relationship. Talking about hometowns and astrological signs opens up the conversation, but the conversation needs to move on in the direction of making the sale.

Another lesson from all this is to keep in mind and regularly remind your staff that shoppers are not all the same. Never keep dumping emotions onto a customer who seems to be getting uncomfortable when you try it out. Research at Universidad Pública de Navarra in Pamplona, Spain confirms what any experienced retailer might suspect: For certain shoppers in the world, emotion sells, but for others, it's a turnoff. How to tell which is which? Monitor the extent to which your shopper uses emotion words themselves.

Also pay attention to the mood the shopper seems to be in when you're dealing with them. Compared to customers who enter your store in a good mood, a customer who enters in a bad mood is less likely to buy items beyond just what they came in for. The mother who comes in for supplies for a sick child is worried, and that worry is one of the reasons the woman will purchase only what's on her list and immediately rush off. The home handyman frustrated by a repair gone awry comes into your store on a mission, not to browse.

As a matter of respect, it is important to provide these customers with signage and staff to get them right to the desired products and then have quick checkout service to get them on their way. Maybe they'll want some conversation to help them feel better. If so, we'll give a listen to the degree we can. But unless they show an interest in chatting, we won't do much talking beyond sincerely thanking them for their business. If they ask for advice, we'll provide it succinctly.

We do this because we know they're in a hurry. But with customers in a bad mood, keeping it brief works for another reason as well: Findings from research at University of Maryland and Yale University indicate that too much talking will lock into the shopper's mind the bad feelings they're experiencing, and those negative memories make it less likely they'll buy from us in the future.

When the shopping experience itself has been responsible for the customer's bad mood, we want to ask questions to find out how to make things right. We then take action, and the customer leaves in good spirits. But when the customer comes into our store already sad, mad, or in other ways not glad, and it wasn't our doing, we don't want to lock in those bad feelings.

We also don't want to be overly cheerful. Customers buy more when they're in a good mood. But customers in a bad mood still buy, and if your customer is feeling grumpy, you'd rather not have the salesperson showing off a much better mood than the customer's mood. Research from the Northeastern College of Business Administration finds that, with one important exception I'll tell you about in a minute, a customer who is in a bad mood is especially unlikely to buy from a salesperson who is obviously in a much better mood than they are.

Many customer service gurus preach that salespeople should exude the nonstop cheerfulness you'd see in Mickey and Minnie Mouse when they're on stage together at a Disney theme park. But if I'm feeling irritated and irritable because I'd much rather be home in bed resting instead of hunting down a cold remedy, my irritation fairly explodes if I'm expected to deal with some salesclerk who fails even to acknowledge my horrible state.

Customers want to spend their money with retailers who will confidently help them solve problems. A way to show that confidence is for the salespeople to project a positive approach. But with the one exception, the salesperson's mood should be just a little more upbeat than the customer's.

The exception? The research says that when the shopper is feeling truly desperate, they have no objection at all to dealing with a highly cheerful salesperson. This is an instance where misery doesn't want company, but instead prefers a can-do attitude. Recall that some customers want their salesperson to be a superhero, who takes responsibility for rescuing them, going above and beyond what most salespeople are able or willing to do. But other customers want a wise salesperson who brings enough experience and a sharp enough mind to see the customer's mood and raise it a little.

⁂

One tool for keeping spirits high is a nice sense of humor. In most circumstances, it's good to kid around, gently and briefly, with the customer. You can give yourself lots of valid reasons not to make jokes with customers: The shopper on a tight schedule doesn't want to take the time to hear you tell your favorite dozen funny stories. Everybody wants their dignity respected, so if the humor takes the form of teasing a customer, you'll lose that sale and probably any opportunity to make a future sale. In many cultures, such as Latino and Japanese, ridiculing a retailer or product that competes with yours is considered offensive.

Then there is a reason which is not as good. You might be concerned that with your gentle, brief humor, the customer might not get your joke. You're afraid they'll feel puzzled, not happy. Here, your fear is unnecessary. Researchers at Georgetown University and University of Washington found that even if consumers didn't fully understand a joke—in the research study, the joke was a pun based on a product's name or features—the consumers still enjoyed the wordplay.

Actually, a joke that isn't immediately understood can be especially effective in making a sale. Research says the shopper's mental energies are taken with trying to figure out the humor, and this distracts the customer from thinking about reasons not to buy. So humor can be useful in moving the indecisive customer to the cashier station. Humor usually relaxes tensions and lifts spirits, both of which enhance the desire to buy. But the partially understood joke actually increases tension temporarily, and the shopper resolves this by making a purchase.

The best humor to use in a sales situation is gentle and informal. To avoid offending, build on what you discover the customer considers to be funny. Make humor a team sport as you volley giggles back and forth.

All of this is more evidence of the importance of tuning into each customer. For example, when customers are ready to make their purchases, move them along. We want our shoppers thinking about their purchases. But if truth be told, we don't want them thinking too hard or for too long. Consumer psychology researchers at Northwestern University and at Radboud University in the Netherlands found that consumers tend to make worse decisions when they ruminate.

RETAILER'S EDGE

Moving customers promptly out of the shopping process can be especially valuable for the five to ten percent of adults who suffer from a certain disorder that I'll describe to you. But first, a question: Does your store take measures to help customers who suffer with disabilities? How about accommodating wheelchairs and holding special shopping events for people with intellectual impairments? Well, what if the disability consists of a compelling urge to keep on buying products or services in self-destructive ways? That problem is called Compulsive Shopping Disorder.

People with CSD tell researchers things like, "It's not that I want it, because sometimes I'll just buy it and I'll think, 'Ugh, another sweatshirt,'" and "I couldn't tell you what I bought or where I bought it. It was like I was on automatic." Doesn't this sound like an addiction? You see, people with the disorder often recognize something's terribly wrong with them.

Compared to your other customers, they are less likely to pay their bills and more likely to return items. Those are a couple of the reasons retailers should care about CSD. In addition, there are mental health professionals who want CSD to be added to the American Psychiatric Association's Diagnostic and Statistical Manual (DSM). If this happens, the legal and ethical obligations for retailers might increase. Think about how, in some states, bars can be liable when their patrons drink alcohol to excess and how Harrah's casinos post notices reading "Gambling Problem? Call 1-800-522-4700."

I'd never suggest to a retailer that they refuse to sell an item to a customer because the retailer suspects the person has CSD. But I would suggest that you and your staff refrain from high sales pressure on customers who seem to be struggling to keep from buying while they're emotionally upset. Instead, help move them quickly through and out of the shopping process.

These days, moving customers through the purchase process is particularly important in the cash/wrap areas. As many retailers are finding, if the customers don't pay promptly, they too often decide to put some products back or just give up and leave. In a troubled economy, sights and sounds at the cash/wrap can trigger needless fretting. Add to the rumination plenty of irritation—the kind that comes from waiting—and it's no surprise when customers flee.

Almost all retailers consider cash/wrap lines as opportunities for added sales. At these stores, lines might snake through shelves filled with chewing gum, batteries, CDs, hair clips, or other items labeled as prime for impulse purchases. I'm all in favor of keeping those items in front of customers. But depending on having people stand in line in order to make sales is bad business. Sprinkle those fun purchase items throughout the store as well as at the cash/wraps.

Around 2007, Loblaw Companies Limited, which is Canada's largest grocery retailer, began gradually rolling out what they call "Clutter-Free Check Out Lanes." Magazines, batteries, and even the impulse-grabbing, high-margin-earning candy bars were gone from the checkout areas. If you want your candy, you buy it in the larger package in the candy section of the main store. The same sort of thing goes for the batteries and the magazines.

Loblaw got congratulations not only for cleaning up the overstuffed cash/wrap area, but also for enabling parents to guide their children and themselves through candy-free alleys, making it less likely that they themselves will end up looking overstuffed. It's true, though, that others said Loblaw was cheating stockholders out of dividends by forgoing the chance to make all those small, last-minute sales when the shopper is waiting in line with cash, check, or credit card ready to go.

Some businesses have taken a more surgical approach to clearing the cash/wrap area, such as removing selected items: Superquinn is one of Ireland's most respected supermarket chains. Feargal Quinn, founder of the business that became Superquinn and author of *Crowning the Customer: How to Become Customer Driven*, was profiled in a December 2007 posting on the *Fast Company* website. Here's an excerpt:

In every deed, focus on persuading the customer to return. Quinn calls it the "boomerang principle." The challenge in building a business on the boomerang principle, he says, is that, in many cases, the option that brings the customer back isn't as quantifiable as the option that maximizes profit on the current transaction.

Take the standard industry practice of stocking candy at checkout counters, which causes a hassle for moms shopping with kids. "They kick up blue murder until the mother buys them something from the display of goodies," says Quinn. While Quinn had hard data spelling out the considerable revenue he would forgo, he had no accountant-friendly evidence on the benefits of removing the sweets. But clearly, removing the displays presented an opportunity to generate repeat business from grateful mothers. "This is where leadership comes in," he says. "It requires courage to take the unquantifiable option." Superquinn ultimately went with the customer-driven choice and banned sweets at checkouts across the entire chain—to an immediate and overwhelmingly positive response.

But again, many highly successful retailers and retailing consultants have a different perspective. Art Freedman, my *Making Money Is Not Illegal, Immoral or Fattening* coauthor, says, "Removing impulse buy items from the check stands is not realistic, real world, or smart. Tell me a great U.S. retailer that does this. Think of the profitability that comes from sales of just batteries at the checkout. Put the candy and gum packs at other places in the store? You'll have big problems with theft. Larger sizes of the candies at other places in the store? What's the impact of that on inventory management?"

It's All About Respect

So what did *you* think, retailer?

Keep in mind that Superquinn and Loblaw are grocery retailers, while Art's store is a hardware/home improvement center. Superquinn has about 23 stores and Loblaw has over 1,000 corporate and franchised stores, while Art has a special interest in the small to midsize retail business. The lesson is that, as with all the other suggestions I make in this book, you'll want to select and adapt.

Anyway, doesn't the clutter in the cash/wrap area make the wait seem to go faster? Shoppers pass the time reading magazine covers and consume mental energy wrestling with themselves about which sweets to buy today. If you are going to shift the product selection purchase sites in your store away from the cash/wrap, either eliminate lineups or introduce ways to make the wait more interesting.

Product information posters. Intriguing ads for stores you've teamed up with. Music that's pleasant to listen to. Those all can work. Harvard Business School research finds that mirrors in waiting lines make the time go faster, since people will get involved in looking at themselves. You might not want to use that one in a Loblaw store, though. There's always the risk that customers would take one look at themselves and start putting the food items back.

༄

Regardless of how you view the Loblaw changes, what can you do today to show respect for your customers by improving the speed of flow through the checkout process? What steps will you be taking next? Should you be training more of your staff to handle cashier duties? Do you have systems set to open cash/wrap stations when waits grow beyond three minutes? Are you able to make use of the wireless technologies that allow staff to carry out part of a customer's payment process while the customer is still in line? Do you announce to customers waiting to pay that help is coming, and do you see to it that those who waited then receive an extra thank you for their business?

This shows respect. Another way to show respect for customers is to use their primary language in advertising, store signage, product labels, and salesperson-customer interactions. Retailers often assume that if a customer is able to speak two languages, the customer is equally comfortable carrying out shopping transactions in either language. But the truth is that the whole personality of the customer and of the transaction might change between languages. Researchers at Baruch College and University of Wisconsin-Milwaukee studied what happened to bilingual Hispanic women as they switched between speaking English and speaking Spanish in American stores.

The researchers found that the women tended to feel more assertive when speaking Spanish than when speaking English. And when these women read Spanish text—as might be used in ads or on signage—the women were more likely to think of acting independently and taking educated risks. An assertive willingness to take educated risks is the sort of thing that can lead to larger purchases and so to more profitability for you.

If your target market includes many people who speak more than one language, here are some tips:

- Look for job candidates who have, in addition to all the other retailing skills, the ability to speak and write your customers' languages fluently.

- Schedule staff so that, at any time, you have at least one salesperson on the floor able to understand and fluently speak the language of almost anyone who comes into your store. Then have the monolingual staff tag team whenever it's needed.

- Train and coach staff to understand the retail shopping expectations of people from different cultures who give you business. This is important not only for closing sales. It is also important for teaming up with the customer to head off misunderstandings about item return policies, how to place a special order, what might appear to be shoplifting, and how to arrange for services offered by the business.

Beyond just spoken and written language, target your customer segments with cultural events. In general, shoppers prefer to buy products from salespeople whom those shoppers see as sharing their distinctive characteristics.

The key word is "distinctive." Members of minorities are more finely attuned to whether a salesperson is a member of that minority than are people who don't consider themselves to be in the minority. Researchers from Stanford University found that African-Americans had more positive reactions to an advertisement with black actors than American whites had to the same sort of ad featuring white actors. Earlier, other researchers had reported that Latino consumers living in Austin, Texas—where Latinos were an ethnic minority—were more likely to trust a Latino salesperson than were Latino consumers living just 80 miles away in San Antonio—where Latinos were an ethnic majority.

You might read this to mean that, to keep your profitability high, you should staff your store with people who share with shoppers what those shoppers see as distinctive ethnic characteristics. Well, yes, that's a good idea, as long as doing business this way affords equal employment opportunities and produces a staff with clear retailing skills, not just certain ethnic, racial, cultural, and language identities. But there's another way to target these distinctive customer segments, and it depends less on the look and sound of your staff: Know what cultural groups in your target market areas do consider themselves to be minorities. Then arrange special events to commemorate their particular cultural celebrations—for example, Cinco de Mayo for consumers of Mexican heritage—or to honor special accomplishments by members of their group—such as Kavya Shivashankar, of East Indian heritage, winning the 2009 Scripps National Spelling Bee.

Well, okay. Maybe bragging about a World Cup win in football/soccer would be better received among your target markets than would bragging about a spelling bee championship.

Respecting different cultures applies even to your choice of colors. Anybody who tells you retailing is exactly the same regardless of culture is failing to pay close enough attention. Yes, the fundamental principles—such as always delivering value for price—are the same. But the devil is in the details. Exercise cultural sensitivity when selecting color schemes for your store décor, product packaging, and media advertising.

There are some universals in how shoppers tend to respond to colors. Reds create excitement associated with fast movement and enhanced appetite. In a McDonald's, red means you eat more quickly, leaving space sooner for the next customer. In a Target store, red means you pile your purchases into the cart more quickly.

On the other hand, blues are associated with leisurely, deliberative shopping. People prefer ads with a backdrop of blue to those with a backdrop of red. American Express named its credit card Blue because their market research showed the color was associated with positive feelings about the future. Perhaps another advantage of blue for the American Express card is in building its brand image as the international card. University of British Columbia research found that blue's appeal crosses cultures widely.

That's not the case with all colors. For example, in most of North America, white brings to mind purity and cleanliness, while in most Asian countries, white is associated with death. Shoppers in India, Japan, and many parts of Europe think of black as a negative color, but in the Middle East, black has generally positive associations.

Even colors with near universal appeal don't work well in every culture. Show consumers from throughout the world green product packaging and you'll hear descriptions like new, organic, healthy, and refreshing. Green has a particular appeal in most Muslim cultures. Except for those consumers with roots in the Middle East, I'm told. For them, I've been advised to avoid green schemes.

∽

Every culture has certain rituals when it comes to being a consumer. Bargaining. Bartering. Gift giving. Disposal of products when they're worn out. All these and many more are governed by standards taught from childhood. Coach your staff to appreciate the importance of those rituals in making a sale.

For example, have you noticed how some shoppers will complain and complain about a product or service that seems ideally suited to the shopper's needs and desires, and then after all the complaining and what seems to be arguing with the salesperson, the shopper will go right ahead and buy the offering? Other shoppers come into your store asking for a specific product and brand, but before buying it—as they'll end up doing—they want to hear about at least a few alternatives, as if to convince themselves they're making the right decision.

And then there are those customers who refuse to buy a product until they can take it out of the packaging and run their hands over it. This last group, not surprisingly, resists making purchases over the Internet, although, according to researchers at University of Kentucky and University of Wisconsin, rituals of the grasp-and-caress crowd can be satisfied with written or spoken descriptions of all the different textures the product has.

The complaining, arguing, searching, and caressing are shopping rituals. I'm sure there are many others you've seen as well, some even more bothersome to busy sales staff than my three examples. As salespeople gain experience, they learn to respect the customer going through the ritual—or if not respecting the ritual, at least staying out of the way of the ritual as much as possible.

Most shopping rituals are quite deep-seated in the personality because they were introduced early in life as the child watched others shop and was coached by parents. Actually, some shopping rituals—such as a need to handle or to smell products—usually have their origins before birth, being hardwired in as the brain develops in the womb.

Never allow your staff to be harassed. But coach your staff to take time to go along with the harmless rituals. Staff might decide not to dance in the store aisles if asked by your customers as the background music plays. But your staff will preserve more sales and make more sales if you all allow your customers to do their own ritualized dances in the store aisles.

RIMinders

- Help customers discover things they have in common—such as birth month and hometown—with your sales staff.

- Provide customers no more than the amount of risk they want.

- By having policies for easy product returns, encourage shoppers to make purchase decisions that feel good to them and don't require prolonged thinking.

- Before using fear, shock, or other negative emotions to motivate shoppers, plan the steps you'll take so shoppers are left at the end with positive emotions, such as relief.

- Keep cash/wrap areas interesting for customers to wait in, realizing that, for many customers, highest interest comes when they don't have to wait at all.

- In advertising, store signage, product labels, and salesperson-customer interactions, use the primary language of your customer and respect their culture and rituals.

5

The Price Is Right

Soon after the breakup of the USSR into Russia and a bunch of other countries, a new, highly entrepreneurial and status-conscious mindset took hold in the motherland. Here's my English-language version of a joke that became popular in Moscow because it played on the mindset changes:

Sergei and Nikolai, two businessmen enjoying prosperity in the changing economic order, happen to see each other in a city shopping district as Nikolai is walking out of a men's clothing store.

"What a surprise to see you here, Nikolai," says Sergei. "The winter weather is so savage, I'd have thought you would have preferred to stay inside your luxurious apartment."

"Ah, Sergei, and I'm equally surprised to see you, and for the same reason. I came to this neighborhood today to buy a new tie, which I have just purchased at this store and put on to wear. I'll open my overcoat for a moment to show it to you."

"Thank you for the brief look, Nikolai. And how much did you pay for this fine tie?"

With a tone of pride, Nikolai says, "This tie cost me 2,500 rubles."

"Oh, Nikolai, how foolish of you. Just directly across the street there, you could have bought the exactly identical tie for *5,000* rubles."

RETAILER'S EDGE

Retailer, what do consumer psychology research findings have to say about pricing your merchandise? Well, for a start, retail pricing is a complex topic. You can find research to support a wide variety of often conflicting approaches. My objective in this chapter is to simplify the complexity into clear recommendations for actions you can take to achieve higher continuing profitability.

As I write these words for you, with the Great Recession of 2008-2009 looking to be easing up, I expect item pricing to be one area where new discoveries will come tumbling out from consumer behavior studies after this book goes to press. I encourage you to regularly check for free updates about pricing by using my RIMtailing blog (www.rimtailing.blogspot.com). In the Labels section along the right side of the blog, click on Pricing. Then when the posts appear, scroll to the bottom for the newest ones.

What we do know now and have known for many years is that with pricing, some truths persevere. For example, people feel less pain when paying the same amount by credit card than with cash. We also know that things are not always what we'd predict at first glance. For instance, a lower price is not always more attractive to the customer. The little joke about Sergei and Nikolai is an exaggeration all right. Still, it's true that in certain circumstances, a higher price brings greater prestige to the purchaser. A distinctively expensive item can let the purchaser show off to others or feel sinfully indulgent.

Here the difference in prices helps the customer make a decision. At the other extreme, there is a pricing technique that moves the customer toward a decision by *eliminating* differences in prices.

Have you ever noticed how restaurants will offer a set of dessert choices, all at the same price? What's going on? Well, those restaurants are making use of consumer psychology: Many diners hesitate ordering dessert. They feel full from having just completed their meal. They know desserts are a danger to diets. But if truth be told, those customers are hankering for dessert to the point of looking for an excuse to order it.

Here's where the fixed price menu comes in. As research at Northwestern University confirms, consumers are more likely to purchase certain types of items when presented with a group of similar alternatives all at the same price. The reason is that parity pricing—which is what this is called—eases the decision process. This technique is used with much more than desserts. Although the prix fixe menu with alternatives for each course is more common in Europe than in North America, prix fixe in the form of parity pricing is seen in at least a few restaurants anywhere you go in the world.

What's of more use to you, though, with what you sell beyond restaurant menu items, is that parity pricing significantly facilitates sales of many sorts of products and services. But only under specific circumstances. Parity pricing is most effective as a selling technique with items where the prospective buyer considers the purchase to be particularly risky. That might be because the buyer believes the price to be high, which involves financial risk. In those retailing circumstances where frugality is honored over frivolity and shoppers hesitate spending money, parity pricing could help ease your shoppers' indecisiveness.

In *Making Money Is Not Illegal, Immoral or Fattening*, the book I co-authored with Art Freedman, we recommend a system for improving profit margins. Here are three of the highlights from the system, which was developed by Art based on his decades of real-world retailing experience:

- Set prices item-by-item rather than by classes of items.

- Set higher margins on items for which you are one of the only sources of supply.

- Set higher margins on products you don't sell often but sell often enough to keep in stock.

RETAILER'S EDGE

Discount prices in order to preserve sales. But don't give up profit dollars needlessly. Unless your chief marketing point is discounts on everything, apply discounts to selected items. Use your sales data to discover where discounts make a difference and where they don't.

Then, since you've one set of items you'll be discounting and another set you won't, sprinkle in discounted items among regularly priced items on the shopping floor. In the place where the customer takes the item off the rack or pulls it from the shelf, surround the discounted items with regularly priced items.

- Finding the discounted items feels to the customer a bit more like a treasure hunt. We don't want to make it difficult for the customer to find featured items. In fact, make it easy with store signage and maybe even aisle locations included in ad circulars. But we want them to feel lucky, since associating good fortune with their shopping at your store makes it more likely that they'll want to come back soon.

- The value of the discount is made more apparent to the shopper by the easy comparison with surrounding items that are not discounted. This, too, adds to the positive excitement.

- When merchandising is done well, the customer is likely to see surrounding items that they want to purchase. Because these other items don't carry the discount, they produce greater profit for you. The customer who has just selected one or more items at a good price now becomes much more likely to say, "With my money savings, I can buy some other items I need at a regular price, and getting them here instead of going to another store gives me another kind of savings—a savings in time. Plus, I'm happy to reward this store with my business for giving me a good deal on the discounted items."

The Price Is Right

❦

As we saw with the story of Sergei and Nikolai, value to your customers can come in ways other than low prices. As another example, if you carry items that are collectibles, customers can turn your store into a shopping destination because you feature complete sets, even when some of the individual items have low turnover for you. Consider this snippet from the *New York Times*: "The weak economy notwithstanding...collectibles buffs paid the highest prices ever...."

Okay, I did leave out a bunch of important details in sharing that quote with you. Specifically, the snippet is pretty old. It's from the January 17, 1991, issue of the newspaper. You see, retailing history does sometimes repeat itself. Rare coin prices, along with the selling prices of many other collectibles, actually rose during the Great Depression. Then in the 2008-2009 economic downturn, the sales of high quality collectibles held up much better than sales in most other retailing sectors. When it comes to collectibles, the urge to possess the whole set means there is less consumer sensitivity to price and more drive in the shopper to buy now.

If you own an antique shop or sell mounted sets of rare butterflies, chances are you've personally benefited from the relatively good profitability in high-quality collectibles. And whatever you sell, think about including in your merchandise mix collectibles like Lladro figurines, Painted Ponies offerings, and the latest annual releases of Christmas tree ornaments. But just as important as this, for any merchandise lines *that are not necessities for the customer*, consider giving them the appeal of collectibles:

- Feature items in groups, each one a distinctive member of the family. If parallel products are available for different age groups, have those items in the same media advertisement and on the same sign. Stock them on the same end cap.

- Introduce new items in the set regularly, at which point you rotate out older versions. This encourages shoppers to buy now.

- Take special orders and publicize resale markets. When your customer is having trouble getting that special item to fill in the missing spot in the collection, help them buy it from you or from a collectors' group. Keep your customers as dedicated collectors.

- If your sales staff suggest the collectible as a gift, you may have a double benefit. Shoppers reduce their price sensitivity when purchasing collectible items, and they're willing to spend more on gift items, even when the gifts will end up being given to themselves.

⁓

Related to the appeal of collectibles, shoppers seem to be getting nostalgic—favoring products which remind them of the past. Are you ready to satisfy that desire? In fall 2009, The Home Depot discarded plans for a purple and brown Christmas in favor of the traditional red, green, and gold. Saks Fifth Avenue said they'd feature gingerbread houses, ball ornaments, suspenders, and cufflinks.

There have always been shoppers who treasure mementoes from years ago, and it's not news that there are merchants who accommodate them with antique toasters, music tracks from old LP records reissued as MP3 downloads, and out-of-print etiquette books. In 2004, Pacific Cycle brought out a redo of the Schwinn Sting-Ray, arousing memories of a bicycle loved by kids growing up a generation before. What is new is the more widespread draw of nostalgia.

Why? I agree with the many other retailing consultants who attribute it in large part to the economic downturn. People began yearning for softer times. Or what they recall as being softer times. The fact is a fair amount of research indicates that when things get really tough, we distort memories of the past to accentuate the positive and eliminate the negative. Following the euphoria exemplified by the Russian tie joke, the economy turned ugly. Many Russians reacted to their economic miseries by buying fashions with hammer-and-sickle logos to remind them of the supposedly good days of dictatorship. And the Chinese are getting downright nostalgic for Chairman Mao Zedong, that fellow who, during the Cultural Revolution, ordered pocket watches and silk scarves to be seized from citizens. By contrast, Mao souvenirs—such as bronze busts ($85 US), snow globes ($6.95), and key chains ($4.25)—are now being featured on Taobao, the Chinese equivalent of eBay.

For as long as the nostalgia appeal lasts, I suggest you set higher retail margins on items that carry this appeal and can be presented to the public as being nostalgic. But don't overstock. I know the buyer psychology pendulum will swing back again. Remember my just using the Schwinn Sting-Ray reincarnation as an example? Well, the Sting-Ray garnered an award as the 2004 Toy Industry Association Outdoor Toy of the Year. But only two years later, Dorel, the Pacific Cycles parent company by then, decided to take a loss of $3.5 million on its remaining Sting-Ray bicycle inventory in order to convince retailers to sell off the bikes.

In that instance, nostalgia was so last year.

For another example of where you can and cannot tweak up prices, let's move on to Italy. Some years ago, Unilever learned a lesson about selling cleaning products to Italian women. It is the women who are almost wholly responsible for home cleaning chores. Unilever knew that Italian women wash their kitchen and bathroom floors about four times as often as American women do and thus, not surprisingly, buy more cleaning supplies. Unilever launched Cif spray cleaner in Italy as a one-swab solution, suitable for all sorts of cleaning tasks. But to their puzzlement, Unilever failed to clean up.

When they asked why sales of Cif were so bad among Italians, Unilever learned that Italian women found it hard to believe a spray cleaner could truly handle, say, kitchen grease. Unilever had failed to note that 72% of Italians own at least eight different cleaning products. Based on what they learned, Unilever changed direction, introducing a set of products, each designed to solve a particular cleaning problem in the home.

That was then and in Italy. What about now and in other parts of the world? A March 2009 study by Information Resources, Inc. (IRI) found that American consumers look for multi-solution products. One customer motivation for multi-solution purchases is so whatever is purchased will be used to full advantage. About 55% of the 1,067 respondents to the IRI survey said they want their cleaning products and personal care products to last longer.

Another motivation is to cut down on the time and transportation expenses of going from store to store. Shoppers now are placing a high importance on item prices. They are willing to travel a bit more for savings. But once they get to a store, they prefer to do lots of their shopping right there. For the retailer who wants to control inventory costs by limiting the number of different products carried, it makes sense to have products that can be advertised as meeting a range of customer needs and desires.

Other research supports the IRI conclusions. Consumer surveys continue to find that shoppers are looking for low prices and for products which promise to solve multiple problems. The surveys say that even when the economy improves, these two trends will continue at reduced intensity. So as a retailer, maintain your stock of multi-solution products.

Because there will be toothpaste shoppers who specifically want cavity protection without the chemicals used for tooth whitening, the toothpaste shelf should carry a specialized cavity protection product. But overall, a toothpaste which promises cavity protection *plus* whitening is likely to sell better than a toothpaste which promises to do just one or the other. And shoppers may have trouble putting into a product category a cell phone with Global Positioning System capabilities. But as soon as shoppers do get comfortable with the idea, the cell phone *without* GPS loses appeal.

Ah, yet there's a wrinkle: Although shoppers are attracted to multi-solution products, researchers at Northwestern University say shoppers tend to believe that, compared to single-solution products, multi-solution products are inferior in each of the capabilities. The product which promises to be a jack of all trades risks being seen as a master of none. The Northwestern University research findings suggest a remedy to the problem, and that remedy is why I'm telling you about all this in a chapter on pricing.

The remedy is for the retailer to charge extra for multi-solution products. The additional cost helps convince shoppers the product can indeed do more. It never pays off in the long run to gouge shoppers with exorbitant prices. But do keep in mind that other trend among shoppers—the search for low prices. Are you trimming profit margins on many of the products you carry in order to keep customers coming? Boosting margins on multi-solution products may be the margin solution for you.

༄

Then once you've identified the items for which customers are willing to pay more, use just-below and rounded-dollar pricing carefully. Setting prices up to just below the next whole dollar can give you extra profit on overall sales. You'd have to look long and hard to find a customer who will buy when the cost is $19.95, but won't buy when the cost is $19.99. Therefore, be sure that the prices on your bin tags and price tags end in $.99, not $.95. Those extra pennies on each sale tally up to big differences over one year's worth of revenues. This is yet another example of achieving a retailer's edge.

But don't go even one penny higher. When a customer is considering how expensive it would be to purchase a particular category of product (like a drill, a baseball bat, or a dress), they'll sense the just-below price (such as $1.99 or $29.99) to be significantly lower than the price which is only one penny more.

The power of the $.99 rule is shown in a study conducted by Kenneth C. Manning, who is a professor of marketing at Colorado State University, and David E. Sprott, who is Associate Dean of the College of Business at Washington State University. They asked people to choose between two ballpoint pens. One pen was priced at *about* two dollars, and the other—an upgraded version—was priced at *about* four dollars. But what a difference two pennies made! When a group of study participants were told the pens were priced at $2.00 and $3.99, fully 44% of the participants selected the higher-priced pen. When another group were presented the prices as $1.99 and $4.00, only 18% chose the higher-priced pen. The people were looking at the figures to the left of the decimal point. A difference between $2 and $3 comes across as smaller than a difference between $1 and $4.

A significant exception to the $.99 price rule is if you want your price points to carry the message that the major advantage of your store is low prices. This could be called the Wal-Mart approach, where prices ending in $.87, $.43, and similar oddities fairly abound. "We've trimmed every last penny off the price," is what you'd be saying.

Another exception to the rule is in ads for products where you have good-better-best choices in a feature comparison format. Once the customer has decided to purchase an item from a product category, they might consider an upgrade. The customer is more likely to choose the more expensive alternative if the prices for the two are presented as rounded-dollar prices instead of as just-below prices. So if the prices on the bin tags are $29.99 and $39.99, a good-better ad would list side-by-side features of each version likely to be most important to the purchaser and then end with, "All this for less then $30" and "All this for less than $40." In the store, the salesperson says, "For only ten dollars more, here are the additional features you would get." With the ballpoint pens in the study by Professors Manning and Sprott, people would be told, "For only two dollars more, you can enjoy these benefits of the upgraded version."

Consumers expect to get what they pay for. I shall now give you an example of that. I'm not sure whether this example is humorous or troubling. I'll let you decide. First a bit of background. You know about the Nobel Prizes. Until this moment, however, you might have been completely unaware of another set of awards, called the Ig Noble Prizes. They are given out each year by the *Annals of Improbable Research* for studies that come across as so odd as to usually draw a chuckle.

And now back to the idea that consumers expect to get what they pay for. The winners of the 2008 Ig Nobel Prize in Medicine were Dan Ariely of Duke University, Rebecca L. Waber of Massachusetts Institute of Technology, Baba Shiv of Stanford University, and Ziv Carmon of INSEAD-Singapore for their research demonstrating that high-priced fake medicine is more effective than low-priced fake medicine in relieving patients' symptoms. The study was published in the *Journal of the American Medical Association*.

If you paid more for your medicine, it works better, even if it turns out that it was not medicine at all, but a fake potion. Yes, consumers expect to get what they pay for.

This leads to another set of issues and opportunities when it comes to offering promotional discounts. Research at INSEAD-Israel and Stanford University confirms that when people buy products or services at what the people consider to be deeply discounted prices, they tend to end up feeling that the product benefits are less than if they'd paid full price. They love having gotten a discount, but they don't have as much love for the product or service.

Consumer psychologists call this the price-quality link. We'd like our customers to be absolutely thrilled with all their purchases from us, so we may be tempted to point out that the discounted item is identical to what the person would have gotten at a higher price somewhere else. But because the price-quality link operates at an emotional, non-rational level, it doesn't easily yield to logical arguments.

In the short term, this can create a nuisance. People who think a product or service is inferior are more likely to request refunds. But in the longer term, it's to the benefit of the retailer to maintain the price-quality link in the consumers' minds. Your staff can say, "We'd be pleased to accept a return and give you a full refund or, if you'd prefer, a credit to help pay for purchase of a regularly priced alternative to the item you bought."

The price-quality link also is useful in another way: The initial enthusiasm when making a purchase often fades over the time the consumer uses and then eventually discards the product. Because the *discounted* product or service begins with more modest expectations, any disappointment the consumer experiences may be less, meaning that good will regarding your store is protected. Certainly deliver full value to every customer. But allowing those customers to believe, "You get what you pay for," can be to your benefit as a retailer. Allow modest expectations of highly discounted products.

When it comes to promotional discounts, let's add another profit maker from the research on the psychology of pricing. Suppose you have one item in your store priced at $222.99 and another item priced at $199.99. You decide to discount each one $11.00. The selling prices are now $211.99 and $188.99. A number of studies have found that customers are more influenced by the *perceived percentage* of a discount than by the *actual dollar amount* of the discount. So which one of the two will be *perceived* by shoppers as a better discount? From $222.99 to $211.99 or from $199.99 to $188.99?

Researchers at Clark University and University of Connecticut found that your customers are likely to feel that the discount from $222.99 to $211.99 is better than the discount from $199.99 to $188.99, even though the first discount is about 4.9%, while the second discount is the better one, at about 5.5%. The fact is that our brains are not good at working with percentages.

Do you need more evidence of that? Okay, here's some, courtesy of researchers at University of Miami and University of Minnesota. Say you want to clear out a line of seasonal merchandise. You apply a 20% discount, and later, when it's not moving well enough, you apply a 25% discount to the sale price. What is the total discount now *off the original price*?

As you struggle to come up with the right answer, I'm thinking that piling even more percentages onto you couldn't hurt. So I'll tell you that when university students were presented with that problem, 59% of them got it wrong. These are university students, and over half of them got it wrong! They added the 20% to the 25% and said the discount was 45% off the original price.

The correct answer is 40%. You take the first discount, the 20%, and that makes the price 80% of the original. Now you apply the second discount—the 25%—to the 80% of the original price. Multiplying 25% by 80% gives you 20%. So we add the two discounts of 20% to produce an overall discount of 40% off the original price.

Yes, I understand. Our minds are busy. Therefore, it's tempting to add the 25% to the 20% and consider it an estimate. Sometimes you'll want to do the calculations for your shoppers so they aren't misled. There are other times that trying to straighten it out could actually add to the shopper's confusion. You might decide to let your shoppers take responsibility for figuring out the total percentage of a discount.

RETAILER'S EDGE

In my opinion, an easier decision is how to set those discount dollar *prices*. I suggest you set discounted prices to end in a $1.99 (for example, $31.99 or $211.99) or $2.99 (for example, $32.99 or $222.99) to maximize the impression on the shopper. There really isn't that much difference between 4.9% and 5.5% in the $211.99 example. The difference looks larger because we pay extra attention to the number to the left of the decimal point. That's another distortion we tolerate because our brains are, after all, only human.

RIMinders

- If there is a category of items that customers often hesitate purchasing because of risks they perceive, move the customers toward purchase by pricing all items in that category the same.

- Otherwise, set prices item-by-item rather than by categories of items.

- Set higher margins on items for which you are one of the only sources of supply.

- Set higher margins on products you don't sell often but sell often enough to keep in stock.

- Sprinkle in discounted items among regularly priced items on the shopping floor.

- Consider giving items the appeal of collectibles and gift items.

- Offer all-in-one multi-solution products and set higher profit margins for these than for single-solution products.

- Unless low prices are your business's major selling point, set prices that end in $.99.

- When offering upgrades to customers, make price comparisons in terms of whole dollar amounts, such as, "For only ten dollars more, here are the additional benefits you'd receive."

- Set promotional discount prices to end in a $1.99 (for example, $31.99 or $211.99) or $2.99 (for example, $32.99 or $222.99).

- Allow the customer to have only modest expectations of the performance of highly discounted products.

- Encourage customers to pay with credit cards.

6

Ease Frustrations About Prices

Having been conditioned by the Great Recession, your shoppers' brains are highly sensitive to increases in prices for items they regularly buy. Shoppers are more likely than usual to assume you're being greedy. Price cuts have become a fact of life throughout retailing. Neiman Marcus, whose CEO bragged in 2005 about the chain's nonstop adherence to "full-price selling," was holding nonstop sales promotions in 2009. In September 2009, the world's largest consumer products maker—Procter & Gamble—finally gave up after months of resistance and announced price cuts across ten percent of its worldwide product lines, pressuring retailers to pass on the reductions to their customers.

In this atmosphere of falling prices, your customers might get highly suspicious when they see prices going up. Therefore, if you find it necessary to raise prices to keep your business thriving, be ready to explain the reasons to customers. Sometimes customers accept the price increases and move on. In other cases, the customers get upset. According to researchers at University of Arizona, Arizona State University, and University of Pennsylvania, the root of the upset is a desire—conscious or subconscious—to punish the retailer. How else to explain a shopper leaving behind a full cart and walking out the door?

What leads to a customer wanting to punish the retailer instead of accepting a price increase?

- Does the customer consider the item to be a necessity? If they believe they must have the item, then even if they can manage to afford the extra charge, they tend to feel trapped when they see a price increase. The answer? When raising prices on items that many customers will see as necessities, use signage to describe less expensive alternatives. Prepare your sales staff to point out the alternatives if a customer complains about a price.

- Is the price increase a surprise? Consider warning customers of upcoming price increases. There's certainly the risk they'll then start looking for other sources for the products they've been purchasing from you. But there's also the opportunity for you to boost sales and to book profits sooner if customers decide to stock up before the cost rises.

- Does the price increase seem unjustified? Have your staff ready to answer questions about pricing. If a customer says, "Why is the price so high?," the salesperson might say something like, "When our suppliers increase their prices to us, we need to pass those increases on to the customers so that we can stay in business and continue both to serve shoppers like you and to employ the people like me."

The explanations most likely to head off customer anger center on the cost of goods to the retailer from the supplier, according to researchers. This means that when selecting the products for which you'll nudge prices upwards, look at ones where there have indeed been increases in supplier charges. Those researchers also found that customer anger is most likely when the retailer's explanations for increases in product costs are in terms of services costs, such as transportation or insurance.

Indignation can lead even loyal customers to pledge to never again enter your store. Or purchase from your vending machine. Some years ago, the Coca-Cola Company was assessing the value of a vending machine which would change the price for a bottle based on the temperature. On hotter days, the price would go up and on cooler days, the price of the Coke would drop.

Well, even the most fervent doomsayers of global warming can't legitimately blame the weather on a guy or gal who just wants a Coke. The outrage from Coke's customers led to the prompt demise of the hot flash vending machine.

But suppose the company said it takes more energy—and is therefore more expensive—to keep a Coke bottle refrigerated on a steamy day than on a chilly day, and that this accounts for the change in pricing. Several studies—both in the laboratory and in stores—indicate that if the amount of the price increase can reasonably be accounted for by a rationale, shoppers will accept the price increase.

Another avenue to easing indignation is to team up with charity. This works best when the charity partner is logically related to the price increase. Suppose major flooding hits a store's target market area, resulting in a demand spike for flashlight batteries. If the store increases the price of batteries, but announces how a portion of the profits will be contributed to the Red Cross, acceptance of the price increase could be a slam dunk.

Also explain price *decreases* to customers when the decrease is more than a short-term promotion. You got a good deal on a large purchase. Or you want to motivate people to try out a new brand. Or you want to help out customers at a time you know money is tight. Be sure what you're saying is true, of course. But at some point, you'll be increasing prices again, so you want to maintain in your customers the impression that changes in pricing are for good reason.

RETAILER'S EDGE

What appears to be at first a complaint about price could be the result of dissatisfaction about something else, or it could be that the customer will keep complaining no matter what you do regarding price and everything else. Respond immediately to customer complaints. But also assess the real reason the customer is complaining and discover what the customer is expecting you to do. If it's not clear, ask: "What do you suggest I do to make things right?"

This redirects the conversation from argument to teamwork. In addition, saying, "What do you suggest I do," instead of, "What do you suggest the store do," relaxes the customer's irritation. The customer is now talking with someone who has the motivation—and, hopefully, the power—to take action.

The customer's proposal might not seem equitable, or even possible. In fact, some consumer behavior experts have been saying that there are customers around who extort retailers by using complaints. These customers make unreasonable demands under threat that unresolved complaints, justified or not, will go viral on Internet social networking sites. These experts point to the case some years ago of the Dunkin' Donuts customer who started a website devoted to complaints about the chain. Dunkin' Donuts ended up buying the site in order to control the exaggerations and misstatements. The site founder's original complaint? The Dunkin' Donuts outlet he went to didn't have nonfat milk for his coffee.

But compare that tale to what happened about three years later: A customer who was outraged about his problems with a Sony product got his complaint website up and spewing. Until Sony resolved the complaint, that is. At which point the fellow converted the website to a depository for Sony fan messages. Research at Case Western Reserve University points out that customers with complaints range from those who just want to have an "I'm sorry" (again, "I'm sorry" is much better than "We're sorry") up to activists who plan to go to the media or to government agencies. When one of your customers complains, assess the agenda.

Then as you assess how you want to respond, keep in mind that protest sites seem to be decreasing in power as product and service review resources. Sites like Yelp—which provides reviews by customers of locally based businesses—will almost surely continue to grow in influence. According to a December 2009 article in *E-Commerce Times*, Yelp has earned a solid reputation as a repository of local business information and reviews. The egalitarianism of Yelp serves a self-policing function. Somebody who posts a crazy comment is likely to be rebutted by a whole bunch of subsequent posters. The upshot: You've less reason to be concerned about extortion by Internet.

Sometimes the complaint about pricing is due to a genuine misunderstanding. In some circumstances, that can be turned to the retailer's advantage. I speak from personal experience as a customer. A while ago, I was shopping for shirts. After finding two of them, I went to the cash/wrap to pay. The salesclerk asked me if I'd brought along the coupon that gave me a third shirt for free when I purchase two. I said, "No, where was the coupon?" She told me it was in the ad that appeared in the prior day's newspaper. Now consider how badly I would have felt if I'd paid for the shirts and then later saw or heard about the coupon.

But my salesperson made sure that didn't happen. She went on to say, "Don't worry. I have coupons right here for you to use. Which shirt would you like as your free third one?" She handed me not just that single coupon, but a whole group of coupons. With my newfound gratitude and excitement, I added two belts, three pairs of pants, and three pairs of socks I hadn't even consciously thought about purchasing before then.

Does each employee on your sales floor and at the cash/wrap have copies of your store's current advertisements, flyers, and circulars? If a customer thinks the ad said something different from what it really said about pricing or terms, it's quick and easy for the employee to straighten out the problem. Having the ad itself takes it away from being customer versus store employee. There's the objective source that both of them can look at.

These misunderstandings are more common than you might think. Researchers at University of Texas at Austin concluded that the average shopper has only about 65% accuracy when recalling what a printed ad actually says. Although the memory of older consumers is worse overall than that of younger ones, when it came to remembering what was in ads, the 65% accuracy rating generally held up across all age groups. Service your customers and your store by having staff carry copies of ads and coupons.

༄

When the agenda does concern item pricing, your overall strategy is to ease the frustrations. You might need to start out, though, by easing the frustrations of your staff and yourself. Is your staff repeatedly dealing with shoppers' complaints and their hard-nosed negotiating? Are you frustrated because you'd like to keep prices lower, but realize your business's balance sheet won't allow it? What about those abandoned half-filled carts, clothing left in dressing rooms, and items returned because the customer discovers a lower price elsewhere?

Frustration eats up needed energy from you and your staff, and frustrated customers are less likely to buy from you. It is in everyone's interest, then, to ease the frustration.

- Describe pricing as subject to change. When your customers and staff know you're regularly reviewing your pricing, looking for opportunities to pass on savings, they are less likely to stay frustrated. Give your staff examples of how you're not keeping all prices high and higher. Then coach your staff to approach customers who are in the area of competitively priced items to say, "Here's an item that might be of interest to you. Notice what we've done to the pricing."

- Give staff and shoppers influence in pricing. Ask for staff suggestions on what items to discount for specials and where to increase margins to balance it out. Point out product alternatives to shoppers so they feel a sense of control, since a sense of control helps wipe away frustration.

Staff members can help by watching and listening for customers asking for smaller sizes of products they are accustomed to using. The sequence might be: The customer complains about the price of a name brand item. The salesperson suggests a house brand that costs less for the same quantity. The customer says they want the name brand, but wish there were a smaller package which would be affordable for them.

Many manufacturers are producing smaller package sizes, often at price points the customer had become accustomed to for the larger size. Customers might—with good reason—complain about getting less product for the same price and still end up pleased with having the alternative available.

In some cases, the product size is smaller, but the value is the same. Under pressure from Wal-Mart—which wanted to save on shelf space taken—laundry detergent manufacturers shrank the size of the container, but also the amount of the product needed for each wash. The product packaging often tells the shopper about the change. In addition, the width of the cap is often greater on the more concentrated product and the label is made more colorful. Research at University of Southern California found that these sorts of techniques leave the shopper with the perception of getting more product in the container.

Do your shoppers want to spend less money by purchasing smaller product sizes? If so, look for suppliers who can help you merchandise that way.

RETAILER'S EDGE

The experience you and your staff gain in resolving frustrations about pricing will help you in responding to other sorts of frustrations, such as those concerning delivery delays. You and your suppliers may be keeping inventory and staffing thinner than in the past. As a result, deliveries of products and services can get behind. To protect repeat business, ease the anger of your customers about delivery delays. Researchers at Arizona State University found that complaints about delays usually come in one or more of three flavors.

- "They don't appreciate the bother this delay is causing me." Allow the customer enough time to tell you, at least briefly, about the bother, and then respond with something that shows you understand the specifics of what the customer said. You might reply, "I understand what a nuisance it causes for you to have to put your project on hold because of the late delivery. How can I make things right?"

- "They're trying to hide something." The customer thinks you're intentionally evil. Reply by emphasizing your ethics. Find out the real reasons for the delay and then tell the customer. You could end up saying something like, "Our regular supplier might be having financial troubles I didn't know about. I'll look into other supply sources. Or would you prefer to cancel the order at this point?"

- "They're making me look bad to others." When the delay in order delivery occurs at the restaurant with business associates around the table, or the news of a special order delivery delay is presented in front of the customer's family, the chance of explosive anger grows. To avoid this, aim to discuss the delay and the remedies one-to-one, retailer-to-customer, out of earshot of the customer's business associates, family, or friends.

Ease Frustrations About Prices

Once again, please note that when the customer is thinking, "*They* are responsible," your response should be "*I* will take care of this." This dissolves anger.

⁓

Price is only part of the formula in consumer decision-making. People are willing to pay more when there is greater value. Think about the value you offer and the values held by people in your target market. Valuing energy saving, for instance.

In your advertising, in your signage, and in your salesperson-to-customer conversations, emphasize your products' energy-saving features. According to an *Advertising Age/ARC* survey, saving energy is a high priority for your shoppers. Today's consumer wants to be thrifty, and energy costs continue to climb. Moreover, consumers want to be socially responsible, and we're told repeatedly that we as a society are wasting too much energy.

There's a third driver behind your customers looking for products which save energy. They like products which use the latest technology, and a sign of state-of-the-art is that the product consumes less energy than older models. The mix of motivations for energy saving is different for different age groups, so you'll want to customize your approach. For teens, the driving force is using the latest technology. Tell them how energy saving prolongs the time they can use a product between battery recharges. For shoppers over age 35, on the other hand, the motivation has more to do with social responsibility. Tell these folks how their purchase helps promote a healthy future.

Emphasizing energy saving means going beyond talking to your customers about it. It means also considering revisions in your store's merchandise mix to pay attention to energy saving as a product feature. It means that when you negotiate with suppliers, you let them know you aim to carry products which conserve energy.

Yes, many shoppers place a high importance on product features other than energy saving. And consumer psychology research has shown that there is a subgroup of shoppers who actually aim to earn social prestige by being wasteful, including wasting energy. For your shoppers who fall into this group, you'll want to adjust what you say. But for most of your shoppers, hearing about energy saving energizes the urge to purchase.

The broader point is to decrease price sensitivity by appealing to a sense of social responsibility. Experts who track consumer behavior have noted a trend as consumers practice social responsibility in their retail purchases. Retailing profits come from anticipating trends, so make contributing to society an integral part of the personality of your business.

Determine the amount of attention you'll pay to social responsibility by analyzing the values of the culture in which your business operates. Research indicates people with backgrounds in collectivist cultures, like those in many Asian and Pacific Island areas, Greece, and Portugal, are more likely to embrace social responsibility than are those who identify with individualist cultures such as Great Britain, Canada, and the Netherlands. A *Time* magazine article about social responsibility among consumers was one of many in the U.S. edition, but it was the cover story in the Asia and South Pacific editions.

Where to begin? Decide how much controversy you want to tolerate. At least at the start, you might choose to take on social responsibility issues that will bring you largely supportive attention. For instance, almost everybody supports reducing the amount of trash we all generate. About half the people responding to a *Time* poll said businesses should place more importance on protecting the environment than on economic growth. Your first social responsibility initiatives might involve exploring ways to sell products that use refillable containers, to favor vendors that minimize unnecessary packing, and to accept old products for recycling.

Somewhat more controversial is the issue of working conditions. There are employers in the world who think that government oversight of employee rights is excessive. But we've little tolerance for exploitation, so you might choose to tell shoppers the ethical ways in which your fair-trade products are produced.

Combining social responsibility with a promotional discount could be particularly powerful. As the 2009 holiday season began, The Home Depot encouraged customers to bring in old power drills, broken or not, to get fifteen percent off on a cordless lithium-ion power drill, touted as good for the environment. Later, if people wanted to bring in their old Christmas lights, they got a discount on an energy-efficient LED set.

And if you're Toys"R"Us, you urged your customers to trade in old cribs, car seats, and other baby items—perhaps part of the estimated one-third of unsafe items never returned to the seller in response to a recall—for a twenty percent credit toward safe items.

- Encouraging trade-ins is a fine way to build your sales. Auto dealers have been doing it for a long while, haven't they? Adding the socially responsible appeal can put it over the top.

- Decide how you will dispose of the trade-ins. In 2009, auto dealers could get Cash for Clunkers from the federal government. But what would you do with a bunch of old broken drills?

- Give the trade-in promotion a time limit and a distinctive name. The "Power Drill Trade In, Trade Up," "Eco Options Christmas Light Trade In," and "Toys"R"Us Great Trade-In" were given a two-week to four-week span. The time limit and distinctive name protect against long-term consumer devaluation of product types purchased with the discount.

- Tell shoppers how their one trade-in will make a difference. Researchers at Georgia State University and Oklahoma State University found that's necessary for maximum influence of an appeal to social responsibility. So in advertising, store signage, and personal selling, say things like how many extra hours of HDTV watching customers get with the energy they'll save using the new Christmas lights.

※

If people miss a chance to buy merchandise you offer at a substantial discount, you'd like them to feel sorry about it. That way, they'll stay alert for the next time you announce a big sales event. After all, the main reason you have sales is to draw traffic into your store so they'll buy not only the substantially discounted merchandise, but also all the items you're selling at higher profit margins. You want people to notice when there's a big sale.

Unfortunately, though, many shoppers who miss a big sale will experience regret in a way that leads them to dislike the retailer and to criticize the merchandise. In a University of Miami research study, people said that a sofa they'd missed purchasing while on sale was less attractive, trendy, and suited to their décor than an objectively equivalent sofa that was still on sale. More importantly, the research found that those missing the sale became less likely to buy anything at all from the retailer. Maybe this is because people were blaming the retailer for what was actually the customer's own fault. Maybe it's because people want to avoid any reminders of the great opportunity they missed.

Fortunately, the research also showed a way to overcome the problems: Offer customers another chance to purchase merchandise on sale. You still want shoppers to come into your store, so the sale should be on what the regretful shopper will find attractive. But if this follow-on sale is on merchandise different from what was offered in the big sales event, the amount of the discount does not need to be nearly as deep as what was available in the big sales event. That's how to avoid giving away profit needlessly while still maintaining the consumer's good feelings about your store and what you're selling.

Those who missed the big sale might be people who are also last-minute shoppers. To help any last-minute shopper justify to themselves the prices they're paying, add the value of ease of shopping and ease of product use. When customers shop for a product or service for future use, they'll pay special attention to the distinctive features. But when they plan to put the item to work soon, they're especially interested in ease of use.

That's true across cultures. Researchers at University of Illinois and Korea University Business School explain that when, for instance, people are looking at word processing software they'll start using in a few months, they give great weight to the range of capabilities of the software. However, if they plan to start using the software within a few days, their primary criterion is ease of learning the software.

The lesson for your salespeople is to remember to ask shoppers how soon they plan to start using the product or service. Knowing this allows the salesperson to focus the information to the shopper on the most effective balance between desirability and feasibility benefits. Whether in advertising, signage, or talk, you don't have time to tell the shopper everything. Home in on what makes a sale which will benefit both the purchaser and your bottom line.

In some cases, you can guess how soon the shopper plans to start using the purchase. Certain items are likely to be last-minute searches. Floral bouquets and hot water heaters come to mind. With these, you don't need to depend on sales staff contact to get the message across. In your advertising and signage, feature ease of delivery, ease of installation, ease of learning, and other angles on ease of use.

There are shoppers who aim to earn prestige by mastering hard-to-use products and services. And many shoppers do want to put their energies into customizing their purchases. But even with those folks, when time is tight for them, be sure they know it can be turnkey.

There's a more general point here: "Sell the sizzle, not the steak." American advertising pioneer Albert Lasker said this in the days when almost everybody agreed that eating red meat was good for you and the sound of sizzling fat made it an even better delight. Mr. Lasker was advising us to tell our shoppers about the benefits of using our products and services, not about the technical specifications.

But now our shoppers want to know about both specifications and benefits. They also want to know how the products and services we sell fit into their system of values. Not just good value for their money, but a good fit with their values. Sell the sizzle *as well as* the steak. Again, sell the values as well as the value.

Sell to the values because what we consume is less important than what we think we're consuming: A team of researchers from France, Australia, and the U.S. told study participants they'd be given either a beef sausage roll or a vegetarian roll to eat. But those tricky researchers had lied to half the participants, who actually were served the other entrée from the one they were promised.

One group of those participants granted a high rating to what they ate, regardless of whether they actually ate the meat or vegetable version, as long as they *thought* it was meat. What does this have to do with values? Unlike the veggie fans, these meat elitists showed up on psychological testing as embracing values of power and strength.

Do you know the values of your target market—what they consider to be especially important in their lives? Is it power and strength? Safety and security? Trust? Perseverance? Playfulness? Craftiness? Friendships? Something else altogether? How well are you weaving messages about those crucial values into your advertising and your salesperson-to-customer contacts?

EASE FRUSTRATIONS ABOUT PRICES

Researchers from University of South Wales in Australia give examples of slogans designed to portray values to match what the target market consumers hold dear: "Don't leave home without it" from American Express to fit into the value of security. "The power to be your best" from Apple to appeal to those who value achievement and influence. "We're number 2. We try harder" from Avis to portray courage or perseverance. "Refreshes the parts other beers can't reach" from Heineken. "It's the real thing" from Coca-Cola. "The ultimate driving machine" from BMW.

I hope that identifying the values of your target market plus all the other ideas I shared with you about pricing make good sense. To be honest with you, one big reason I hold that hope is because I want to have earned permission from you to finish off the chapter with two tactics that, although solidly supported by research and having to do with pricing, sound weird and weirder.

- For cash purchases, give change in smaller bills unless the customer asks otherwise. University of Iowa research suggests that when your store is associated in consumers' minds with small denomination bills, customers are more willing to spend their money with you.

- If it looks as if the customer doesn't want to think about the price because it's painful, avoid mentioning the price—but if asked, say the price sloooowly. Researchers at HEC School of Management, Paris and at University of Pennsylvania find that this makes the shopper less sensitive to the price. So if the price is $148.29, instead of saying, "one forty-eight twenty nine," take a deep breath and say, "the price of this item is one hundred forty eight dollars and twenty nine cents," carefully enunciating each syllable. Maybe this tactic works because you don't notice the sour taste of the medicine as much when it goes down a very little bit at a time.

RIMinders

- Prepare your staff with what to say to explain price increases and non-promotional price decreases to customers in case the staff members are asked about the changes.

- Coach staff to discover if a complaint about price is due to a misunderstanding of an ad or really a complaint about another issue altogether.

- Ask for staff suggestions on what items to discount for specials and where to increase margins to balance it out.

- When raising prices on items that many customers will see as necessities, use signage to describe less expensive alternatives.

- Consider warning customers of upcoming price increases.

- Decrease price sensitivity by appealing to a sense of social responsibility.

- For cash purchases, give change in smaller bills unless the customer asks otherwise.

- If it looks as if the customer doesn't want to think about the price because it's painful, avoid mentioning the price—but if asked, say the price slowly.

- Continually identify and implement ways to deliver greater value to customers in ways that preserve healthy profit margins for your business.

7

Make the Total Purchase Bigger

What better way to increase your profitability than to increase the total of each customer's purchase? To accomplish that, you could make add-on sales, show the customer the value of upgrades, or both. You're aiming to increase the line items per transaction and increase the dollar amount of the average transaction. Consumer behavior research findings suggest some effective tactics for doing these.

I'll describe those tactics to you in terms of ways of looking at your shoppers. In Chapter 3, I'd told you about one way—what I'm calling the Jungian categories of Superhero, Coach, Guru, Playmate, and Rascal. Each of these five archetypes has distinctive expectations of your staff. In this chapter, you'll read about the Jungian theory again very briefly plus other ways the research findings suggest you look at your shoppers. They're all different. As you read through them, I think you'll find that some make more sense to you than others. Those that make the most sense are the ones you and your staff should use.

But there's another item of business to take care of first: A primary rule for making total purchases bigger is to be sure you don't stand in the way of the customer who does want to buy more or wants to upgrade. A common error at the point of purchase is to answer customer questions in such a negative way that the customer loses any enthusiasm they arrived with.

After your staff members have heard the same customer question a dozen times, do they look the next customer who asks that question straight in the eyes and say, "Good gosh. Don't you know *anything*"? Well, okay, maybe not, but I'll bet your staff who are asked the same question repeatedly can forget how important it is to welcome customer questions enthusiastically. After all, questions signal the customer's interest in making a purchase from you.

Whenever you answer a customer's question with enthusiasm, expect the customer to become enthusiastic. If that doesn't happen, analyze why. Maybe you misunderstood the question. Maybe you've not noticed whether the customer wants your answer to consist of product specifications or general reassurance. According to researchers at Stanford University, University of Utah, and University of Iowa, customers usually want specifications pre-purchase, but after making the purchase, they're usually seeking reassurance.

In most cultures and situations, a smile is an essential component of enthusiasm. Unfortunately, some people otherwise qualified to do retail sales have great difficulty putting a smile on their faces or in their tone. People like this who happen to be on your staff don't belong on the sales floor until they become able to project happiness.

The absence of a smile and the short discourteous answers could be because the staff member is burned out on their current job. They are tired of the same routine with the same job duties day after day, and their enthusiasm is long gone. As you'd expect, that's more likely with the long-term employee. In some cases, the solution is to guide the employee into retirement from working for you. In most cases, though, you'll probably choose to keep the employee. Here the effects of burnout might disappear if you move the employee to a different department, where they'll be energized by getting a whole new set of questions.

If circumstances are such that you find it best to keep the employee in the same place on the sales floor, try out one or more of the following three techniques organizational psychologists have found useful in combating burnout:

MAKE THE TOTAL PURCHASE BIGGER

- Remind the employee of the specific ways their enthusiastic job performance contributes to the success of the business. "When you show an interest in the customer, as I saw you doing just now with that family, the customer wants to stay in our store longer and come back again sooner."

- Expand the job responsibilities surrounding the sales task and introduce more variety in job tasks. "I'm especially interested in making add-on sales with products newly introduced in the store. I'd like you to learn more about each of those new products in your department, and then I'll ask you to do some training about the products in our weekly staff meetings."

- Provide more frequent feedback. We sometimes take the job performance of senior employees for granted. Because the retailer's time is limited, they put all their coaching into work with new employees or staff whose performance is falling far short. These retailers can forget that every staff member thrives on continuing feedback about their job performance. In fact, regular feedback can have a more powerful effect on the employee whose performance is falling a little bit short than on the performance of an employee who is far from adequate.

༄

Sales staff enthusiasm works the world over in increasing the amounts customers spend. But the way that enthusiasm should be displayed does depend on the culture and the situation. When Wal-Mart first opened stores in Germany, employees were expected to greet customer questions with a smiling, enthusiastic welcome. Shopper analyses showed that the customers thought this type of enthusiasm fit better with an Oktoberfest beer parlor than with a Wal-Mart shopping fest. The customers felt the sales help were flirting with them. It was time to keep up the enthusiasm, but tone down the smiles.

Once you've taken care of the staff enthusiasm issue, move on to other techniques for boosting shopping cart totals at the cash/wrap. To start, get customers thinking about how much money they can afford to spend in the long run, not just right now. Researchers from Princeton University, University of Chicago, and Digitas-Boston surveyed people entering a grocery store. About half the number of shoppers were asked, among other things, questions about the contents of their wallets. This nudged their thoughts to the money they could spend in the short term. The rest of the shoppers were asked instead about the different types of financial accounts they had in their investment portfolios, including checking and savings accounts. This got those shoppers thinking about the long-term big picture.

What difference did it make? The second group spent 36% more on their shopping trip than did the first group. Notice how easy it was to have those customers thinking in ways that resulted in them spending, let's say, $136 instead of $100. A question about financial accounts instead of about wallet contents was enough to do it.

But how can you use this information? Customers coming into your store won't welcome being stopped to answer a survey before you let them make their purchases. And if your sales staff who welcome the shopper start out by asking, "How much do you have in your savings and checking accounts?," I think the chances are good that the shopper will gallop out your store's front door with their checkbook, wallet, and credit cards.

What are ways you can gently bring the customer's mind into a longer-term perspective on spending their money? How about stating prices not just as the total, but also as the cost per month over the expected useful life of the product?

How about offering extended payment terms? What else will work for *you*?

Along with appealing to a longer-term perspective, build shopping cart totals by appealing to a perspective of fun. Stock fun items throughout your store. Researchers from New York University and University of Pennsylvania found that when people put a healthy food item into their grocery shopping cart, they become much more likely to select a *fun* food item next.

In choosing the fun food item, the shoppers are still interested in the nutritional value, but from the opposite point of view. They might very well be selecting the fun item because it's *not* nutritious. This sort of thing is true for all kinds of merchandise beyond food items and for e-commerce as well as store purchases. A shopper who makes a good, sober purchase decision is ready to buy an item that's mostly for fun.

When your customer is looking around for fun items, you'll want to be sure you make those items easy to find. The best way to do this is to have fun items displayed throughout the store and throughout the website. More than this, whenever a customer makes the decision to buy a highly sensible item, sales staff should offer the customer a follow-on sale of a fun item in the same or a related product category.

Offer the fun item in a similar category because shoppers like the items in stores to be arranged with some scheme. But shoppers also like variety within a product category, and the fun items clearly can add variety. Researchers from Columbia University and University of British Columbia found that the sort of variety provided by fun items even helps customers in crowded stores to feel better about their shopping experiences.

Next to the hot water heaters, stock T-shirts carrying the motto "Plumber in Training. No Drips Allowed." Across the aisle from where you sell the office desks, feature desktop trinkets designed to hold photos of family and friends. Alongside the high-priced weed killer, have some flamboyant flamingos and other colorful lawn decorations.

RETAILER'S EDGE

For each of *your* product categories, what are some items you can include that are there mostly because they would be fun for the customer to have, or even just fun to consider purchasing? How can you display those items to project the fun, the excitement, the humor?

The more general point has to do with one of the most thoroughly researched facts in consumer psychology: Every customer walking into your store is somewhere along a dimension that at one end is called prevention-focused and at the other end is called promotion-focused.

- Prevention-focused shoppers put top priority on products and services which help them avoid losing what they have now. They want advertising, store signage, and salespeople to tell them how the product will protect them. In my version of Jungian terminology, these shoppers are most likely to want a Superhero.

- Promotion-focused shoppers put top priority on products and services which help them gain more than they have now. They want advertising, store signage, and salespeople to tell them how the product will give them benefits they would otherwise miss out on enjoying. In my version of Jungian terminology, these shoppers are most likely to want a Coach.

Every expert I know about says that almost all consumers will, on a specific shopping trip, be near one of the two extremes. Only a few consumers will come into your store with a 50%/50% mix of prevention focus and promotion focus. A number of experts go beyond this. They say that a person usually stays either prevention-focused or promotion-focused not just for that specific shopping trip, but well beyond that, to last over the course of their adult lifetime as a shopper.

To help your customers make decisions they'll be happy with—so they will buy more—use sales strategies which fit the individual's prevention/promotion category. In one study conducted at Northwestern University, people who said they'd end up happiest when they ate healthy foods were offered the choice between an apple and a chocolate bar. But wait! Before being offered the choice, each person took a psychological test to find if they were prevention-focused or promotion-focused. Later, some of each type were asked to answer a prevention-focused question, "What are some of the things you can do to avoid anything that could go wrong?" The rest—again some from each type—were asked a promotion-focused question, "What are some things you can do to make sure everything goes right?" Immediately after that, the apple and the candy bar were presented.

When the question the person was asked fit the type of shopper they were, they selected the apple about 80% of the time. But when the question the person was asked was opposite of the type of shopper the person was, they selected the apple only about 20% of the time.

The lesson for retailers? Assess if the shopper you're dealing with is mostly prevention-focused or mostly promotion-focused. Then ask your questions of the shopper and present your selling points to fit that individual's focus. You won't have the benefit of administering a psychological test to separate the prevention-focused from the promotion-focused customers. You and your staff members will do the diagnosis by listening to each customer. Discover if the customer is primarily interested in avoiding a loss of what they have now or primarily interested in gaining more than what they have now.

⁓

Still another way to categorize customers is into mission shoppers and possibilities shoppers.

- When you watch shoppers entering your store—or track their browsing patterns on your website—do you notice how some of them are clearly on a mission? They go right for a particular item and, if the value is right, they want to buy the item as soon as possible.

- Other shoppers love to look through the possibilities. Even if they've a specific item in mind, they enjoy digesting the alternatives.

Are men more likely to be mission shoppers and women more likely to be possibilities shoppers? Yes, at least when it comes to clothes, according to some Stanford University researchers. In general, men come for clothes out of necessity, and when they do bullet on into the store and ricochet into the men's clothing department, it's with a targeted purpose in mind. On the other hand, women are more likely to circulate around so they can socialize, analyze, and discover what's new.

Be grateful for your mission shoppers. They're spending money with you and they don't waste your time. But also move mission shoppers into being possibilities shoppers. This helps improve your profitability because the longer the shopper spends with you, the greater the chances you'll make a large sale. The possibilities shopper buys more items and is more likely to upgrade to higher-quality items.

- Do your store/website displays and merchandise arrangements stimulate browsing and upgrading?

- Are your store aisles wide enough for customers to stand in front of the merchandise without getting in the way of other shoppers?

- Are your staff strong in recognizing the difference between a mission shopper and a possibilities shopper so each shopper's needs can be met superbly?

Make the Total Purchase Bigger

Do mission shoppers remind you of sports stars running down the field to win the championship game? If so, I'll take it as a good transition to telling you about a sales builder from the world of sports: For some customers, shopping gives the same emotional charge as watching an exciting sports event. A University of Oregon study of football game attendance suggests some ways you can keep up the thrills and pack the stadium—I mean, your store.

The researchers found three varieties of sports fan motivation:

- Die-hard fans. These football fans are committed to the team and love the sport of football. These store shoppers love the game of shopping, and they're dedicated to doing it with you. Keep feeding them information about the history of your business. Have staff spend time talking with them. Post pictures of the team. Give them plenty of notice about upcoming changes so they feel they're in the know. Distribute business cards and special event announcements for them to pass on to their friends. Sell items carrying the store logo.

- Fair-weather fans. These football fans like to cheer for the winners, and they'll switch who they cheer for if games get dull. These store shoppers get their excitement from looking at the latest developments. If it's electronics, they want to be the experts on the newest technologies. If you carry clothing, they want to try on next month's big thing. If it's groceries, they're into the Food Network trends. These shoppers are much more likely to switch stores than are the die-hard fans. Keep them excited by regularly introducing new items and new ways of presenting your classic items. They like to be around winners, so use signage and conversations to tell them how your store is better than the alternatives.

- Tailgaters. These football fans are there for the camaraderie. These store shoppers get most excited about the social experience. Hold special events in and around the store. Have places in the store where small groups can exchange critiques. Give discounts when a group of shoppers purchase together.

When people shop in groups, each shopper's cart tends to ring up a higher total than if those same people had shopped alone. This is especially true for female shoppers and is the principle behind Avon and Tupperware parties. It also holds for in-store shopping, and now some businesses are finding it works even in the online world: Cultural arts retailer Novica is using Sesh to allow customers to discuss the jewelry, paintings, home décor, and clothing they're thinking of buying. Fashion retailer Charlotte Russe is using ShopTogether to allow small groups, each person working from their own computer, to collaborate in making shopping decisions. ShopTogether user features include "Show your friend what you are looking at," "See what your friend is looking at," and "Chat with your friend as you shop together."

Charlotte Russe and Novica are great examples of where group shopping is at its best. With fashion purchases, shoppers are keenly aware of the social risks as they make their selections. Learning what others have to say reduces the downside risk. It also means that if a woman and a few of her close friends all walk into a party wearing the same outfit, it's more likely to have been intentional, not an embarrassing accident.

With cultural arts purchases, there are background stories which add value to the items. When my buddies and I are all looking at the Novica Axe Carnaval mask at the same time, one might reminisce with a story of his experiences in Brazil at the time of Carnaval and another might share how the Axe mask reminds him of an African mask he has hanging in his office. Whatever the channel for shopping—home party, in-store, online—build sales by making it fun for customers to invite their friends to shop along.

༄

Special events can motivate shoppers to invite their friends to come along, and even the shoppers who arrive at the store alone can catch the enthusiasm of group shopping once involved in the special event. An example of a grand special event occurred on a Thursday night in September 2009. Thousands of mid- to high-end fashion stores held special events under the title Fashion's Night Out. The objective was to build store traffic which would lead to increased sales. Although FNO was centered in New York City, the thousands of participating stores were in other areas of the U.S. and in Brazil, Britain, China, France, Germany, Greece, India, Italy, Japan, Russia, Spain, and Taiwan.

The payoff from a special event may not be immediate. It might be a matter of the group excitement planting a seed which will sprout later. A *New York Times* article about the September 2009 FNO quoted one shopper as saying the event was, "effective in terms of speaking to my aspirations and desires, but maybe not my pocketbook." When asked about sales results from the event, Macy's executives seemed to be far from effusive: They said profits from the event would at least cover the expenses of keeping eight Macy's stores nationwide open a few hours later than usual.

You don't need to be a high-fashion retailer to benefit from a special event. Say you sell cat food in New York City instead of what comes down a New York City catwalk. Well then, consider that Meow Mix Wet Pouches were launched in the Big Apple at events in which consumers were encouraged to bring their cats for taste tests.

Research at University of Colorado and Columbia University Business School suggests that the nature of a special event should take into account whether shoppers perceive the items for sale as routine or risky purchases. For items carrying financial or social risk or if you expect your target audience to be mostly prevention-focused, emphasize how-to-use-it information in the special event. For items that are fairly routine purchases or if you expect your target audience to be mostly promotion-focused, special events should emphasize free trials of small samples. Don't offer free samples of regularly sized items, since research says this would make it less likely the customer will want to purchase the fully priced item in the future.

A final point about special events: Never let the crowds or the activities get in the way of your special event participants easily buying merchandise from you. People might not want to stay around or wait until the end of the event to make a purchase.

A family that shops together is a special kind of group, providing special opportunities for adding to a sale with more items than the shopper first intended to buy. The customer decides on one item and then the salesperson suggests others that fit together with that item in the same way that members of a family fit together. If a woman comes in with her daughter and buys a casual dress for herself, the salesperson asks the woman if she'd like to go on to shop for a casual dress for the daughter.

It's not just with clothing. Ask the man shopping for fishing gear for himself if he'd like to look at fishing equipment for his wife and children who are there with him. And it goes beyond items to be used by different family members. Research done at University of Toronto and University of Chicago suggests that a shopper who comes into the store to purchase a large first aid kit is more likely to buy a second kit if the two kits are described as fitting together like a family. "Keep the bigger kit in your auto and carry the littler one on hikes."

This emotional appeal to the shopper is not the same as, "You bought the paint, did you remember the brushes and sandpaper pads?" It's more like, "Would you also like some smaller sandpaper pads so the kids can participate in the project?" It's for items that have family associations for the shopper and where you carry a variety of product sizes.

Culture makes a difference. Shoppers raised in Latino cultures, which place special importance on the family, will be more open to add-on sales of a family of products than shoppers whose cultural backgrounds are less family-oriented. Whatever the culture of your target markets, though, are your staff members recognizing opportunities to sell families of products and then selling all in the family?

༄

To get the most profitable results from encouraging group shopping, keep in mind that although the total of the customers' purchases tends to be greater than when they shop as individuals, their memory for what a salesperson tells the group tends to be inferior. When in a group, customers forget what they are told more than do shoppers you address as individuals. Repeat the information more often when selling to a group of friends or family.

Of course, you don't want to offend your shoppers, and repeating the same information word-for-word could offend—or at least bore—any shoppers in the group who *did* understand you the first time and *did* remember what you said. To lessen the chances of offending, look at the different members of the group as you repeat the information. Catch the eye of each of those who appear to you to have not understood.

With some product information, you can repeat the message in different ways. Tell the group of shoppers verbally. Then show them written material that repeats the information. Next, demonstrate your points by showing the shoppers what you mean. And check for understanding by asking the shoppers their opinions about what you've said. Multichannel teaching always helps improve learning.

Because of the tendency of group shoppers to forget, it's especially valuable there.

There are purchase situations where the forgetting can turn out to be useful. Researchers from Indiana University found that when members of the group are presented brand information, it disrupts memory for the brand's competitors in that product category. The effect is strongest when the group is collaborating in making the purchase decision. If you've decided that a particular brand would best serve both the needs of the group of shoppers and the profit potential for you, the retailer, repeat information about that brand, but not about the competitors.

Whether dealing with a group or with individual shoppers, make add-on sales by offering customers a basic model plus options at extra cost. Offering stripped-down models with the option of add-ons has always been a great way to woo entry-level customers. But the appeal of add-on accessories can go beyond this. Researchers from London Business School, Harvard Business School, and Duke University found that when a shopper learns that add-on accessories, such as a tripod for a camera, are available, the shopper's opinion of the basic product becomes more positive. This increases the profit potential.

The researchers found that shoppers are more comfortable when downgraded versions of products are available for sale. This might mean:

- Have a bare-bones version of the product or service, a smaller package or a sample to try out to start.

- Show upgrades on the shelves or make them easily available via special order.

This does not mean the customer necessarily ends up purchasing the bare-bones, downgraded model. It is the *availability* of downgrades and upgrades, not the *purchase*, which improves the consumer's ratings of the basic product and relaxes the shopper's fear of buying the whole pie at

Make the Total Purchase Bigger

once. Once the customer says yes to the slice, they're more likely to end up wanting the whole thing at some point.

But be careful to distinguish product *accessories* from product *features*. It is add-on *accessories*, not add-on *features*, which improve the perception of the product. Offer a 32MB memory card for that base 64MB camera and the consumer's evaluation of the base camera goes *down*.

Add-ons of all sorts appeal to the loads of customers who like to customize. The NikeId page invites you to "Customize your game" by selecting add-on designs and colors. And at a Mars site, you can add on to M&M candies your messages and photos, "as long as it doesn't leave a bad taste in anyone's mouth," which does seem to be a sensible requirement when it comes to M&M's.

From another angle, offer add-ons because many consumers are learning to start simple, even if they can afford the fancier version. Philips Electronics says that more than 50% of Philips products which shoppers end up returning have absolutely nothing wrong with them except that the purchaser couldn't figure out how to use all those features they'd bought. The advice for retailers: Merchandise and price your items to feature both basic models and packaged upgrades. Whatever the customer buys, you can follow up in a few months to let them know about the add-ons you have for sale.

༄

Among selling techniques considered tried and true is the foot in the door. The traveling salesman on the front porch with the perfect timing of an expert senses when the lady of the house is about to say no, and at precisely that point offers a combination of merchandise and cost which can't be refused. Once the lady says yes—or even maybe—thereby keeping the door from being slammed shut on the salesman's foot, the sale is built with upgrades and additional items.

In store-based selling, you'll benefit from refining the technique. The first objective is getting the customer to say yes. In a wide variety of studies, it's been found that once the prospect says yes, they're more likely to continue saying yes. Research findings from University of Amsterdam say that even getting the shopper to nod seems to help, as long as a nod means yes in that person's culture.

Another merchandising tactic for boosting sales is to stock larger package sizes. Given a choice among littlest, medium, and biggest package sizes, some food shoppers—usually the promotion-focused shoppers—pick the biggest one, while others—prevention-focused shoppers—pick the medium size. If your shoppers have the money to spend and if it is to the benefit of your shoppers to purchase more, you can increase the package sizes they buy—with the added profit this brings—when you increase the package sizes of your littlest, medium, and biggest versions.

An example of this came from Duke University researchers' look at purchases of soft drinks at fast-food restaurants. When the littlest-medium-biggest choices were 12-ounce, 21-ounce, and 32-ounce cups, promotion-focused shoppers most often selected the 32-ounce version—the biggest size. When the choices were supersized to 21, 32, and 44 ounces, promotion-focused shoppers selected the 44-ounce cup—the new biggest size.

At the other end, prevention-focused shoppers liked the 21-ounce cup—the size choice in the middle—when the choices were 12, 21, and 32 ounces. But when the choices were 21, 32, and 44 ounces, the prevention-focused shoppers liked the 32-ounce size—the new medium size. The 32-ounce drinker moved up to being a 44-ounce drinker, and the 21-ounce drinker moved up to being a 32-ounce drinker.

This power to switch shoppers to larger package sizes works better with soft drink cup purchases than with, let's

Make the Total Purchase Bigger

say, furniture purchases But it works for more than just food retailers.

Will dieters be angry that all you offer are the larger food package sizes? Well, it turns out that you actually might be helping out the dieters. A group of researchers in Portugal and the Netherlands say that dieters find it more comfortable to exercise self-control in their eating after purchasing large package sizes than small package sizes of the same foods.

~

Of course, give them a whiff of the delicious food, and their control against buying more could quickly fade.

Is your real estate agent holding an open house in hopes of selling your place? Don't forget to put those chocolate chip cookies in the oven! Oh, and then turn those ceiling fans to low so the delicious aroma stays in circulation.

A classic finding in consumer behavior research is that aromas influence buying behavior. When a smell hits our brain, it starts out its processing in the limbic system, which is one of the most primitive parts of the brain. People make decisions instantly and unconsciously based on smells. As it happens, the chocolate in those cookies gives an extra kick because the brain neurons it sets off are associated with sexual pleasure.

The most natural uses of odors are in providing the consumer a sample of the product: the scent of bread in the grocery store bakery or the smell of a cleaning product in the janitorial supplies shop. According to *Forbes* magazine, the Hard Rock Hotel in Orlando, Florida began pumping a waffle-cone and sugar-cookie bouquet into the air to lead shoppers towards an out-of-the-way ice cream shop in the facility. But don't restrict yourself just to opening a package of an odiferous product and waving it around.

RETAILER'S EDGE

The Abercrombie & Fitch store on Fifth Avenue in New York City has gained a certain fame for the pleasantly distinctive fragrance you consistently encounter when entering. According to consumer psychology guru Martin Lindstrom, British Airways pumps an aroma named Meadow Grass into its business lounges to help you forget you're in a stuffy airport. And I've come across reports about a pilot study at the Las Vegas Hilton concluding that gamblers exposed to a certain fetching odor pumped 45% more money into the slot machines than those not exposed to the odor.

Now don't get me wrong. Smell's not enough to close the sale all by itself. Even the best perfume or cologne has to be backed up with the goods in order to move a relationship forward. But a faint smell does set the groundwork.

The key word in that last sentence is "faint." Make the odor of cleaning liquid, perfume, or even cookies too strong, and the *customer* might *faint*. And then there are the smells in a store that at any strength will chase off shoppers. How about the air around a dirty restroom?

As you and your staff walk the aisles, breathe freely and deeply. Your store has one chance to make a first impression. Be sure that first impression is rosy.

Unless your shoppers are allergic to roses.

Then once we keep the nose happy, let us stimulate the sense of touch. Researchers from University of California-Los Angeles and University of Wisconsin found that having an undecided customer hold a product makes the customer much more likely to end up buying it. Not only that, but the customer is willing to pay a higher price for the product. The power of touch is so strong that at the start of the 2003 holiday shopping season, the Illinois state attorney general's office issued a warning to shoppers to be cautious around retailers who encourage them to hold objects and imagine the objects as their own when shopping.

Let's not mislead customers, but let's also use research findings to make more money. Touch sells products. Now, if a product is unpleasant to touch, a feel doesn't result in a

Make the Total Purchase Bigger

feeling to buy. So check with your customers whether the merchandise you stock is actually nice to hold. If it isn't, be sure at least the packaging is. It's better to check with the customers than make the decisions by yourself because the degree of pleasantness often depends on an individual's own memories and associations.

Actually, any unpleasantness about touching might have more to do with the recent past than the distant past. When you push a shopper to fondle the merchandise, you need to think about who will be coming along next. Researchers at University of Alberta, University of British Columbia, and Arizona State University verify what most of us would have predicted: Customers have less interest in an item on a rack or shelf when they're thinking about who else has touched it. They feel disgusted at the idea the product could be contaminated by other shoppers.

Although that finding isn't really unexpected, the researchers did discover a few intriguing details about what causes and doesn't cause the disgust: First, the closer a customer is standing to the item when it's being handled and the more people the customer has seen handling it, the more likely it is that the customer will reject the item. However, if a fair amount of time has passed since the item was touched, the customer no longer rejects the item. Second, the disgust is worse if there is evidence of product damage, but the disgust develops even if there is no visible evidence the product has been damaged.

Based on all this, here are a few ideas for maintaining the selling advantages of the touching while avoiding the sales-disruptive effects:

- Adjacent to, but separate from, shelving and racks that hold the items to be purchased, have sample items that can be handled by the customer.

- Have staff frequently refold, repackage, and reshelve in order to remove cues of product contamination.

- Space out items on racks and shelves rather than have them tightly stocked. (This is a technique I also mention when talking about product recalls.)

- In advertising and signage, avoid showing pictures of people handling the product, since it can be a cue that sets off disgust. (This is a technique I also mention when talking about comparison advertising.)

- Provide hand sanitizer dispensers throughout the store.

In the era of the H1N1 virus—better known in the U.S. as swine flu, although people don't catch it from pigs, and in some other parts of the world as California flu, no doubt in tribute to the debauchery in which my homies wallow—it's not just the *merchandise* which is of concern to shoppers.

Suppose my wife, Irene, were to stop at your store to do some shopping with you. As she walks over to get her cart, she sees a customer sneeze onto the handle of the one Irene was aiming for. Irene selects another cart, but then starts thinking, "I have no idea if anybody sneezed on this one."

Protect your customers. Don't take away their shopping carts, for goodness sakes. Ever since Sylvan Nathan Goldman received his patent for the shopping cart on March 15, 1938, conventional wisdom has been that you boost sales whenever you get a shopping cart into the hands of a customer. But how about putting a disinfectant wipe dispenser right by the carts?

In ads and displays, tell your customers you're protecting them. Use a message like, "We want you to stay healthy. Our complimentary wipe kills 99.9% of germs on shopping cart surfaces." You're saying, "We care about you," and your saying that earns you a lot.

Include a waste basket for used wipes, and be sure the waste basket is emptied frequently. Then turn this into a marketing opportunity. Have a display nearby where shoppers can buy packages of disinfectant wipes from you to take home with them.

And now back to the sense of touch for one final swipe: In an article published in the mid-1990's, a pair of researchers at Texas Tech University reported that shoppers became more likely to handle the bottles in a wine store when the brightness of the interior lighting was increased. Three subsequent events aroused interest in that finding among retailers who wanted to use consumer psychology research to build their profits.

First, other researchers had been finding that when customers handle a product, they're more likely to buy it. Retailers might think things work like this because products such as clothing and linens feel so good that once we get our hands on them, we don't want to let them go. But do wine bottles feel so good to the touch? Well, yes, if getting the right bottle into our hands builds our associations with the sensual pleasures of drinking the wine. If brighter lights cause customers to handle the product—all sorts of products—we've another promising tactic to build sales.

For many retailers, a second event was recognition that the age of their customer base is increasing, and older shoppers feel welcomed by brighter lighting.

The third event was the arrival of the first outrageous invoice from the power company. If we're going to jack up the wattage of the lighting system, at least some of the profits from added sales could be consumed by the utility bills. The answer is to use accent lighting. You don't need to up the wattage of the whole place. In fact, accent lighting will work best to direct attention to particular areas and items if you pull back on the overall brightness of the store lighting. You could possibly end up reducing your costs. That would be a nice addition to making each customer's total purchase bigger.

RETAILER'S EDGE

RIMinders

- Maintain the enthusiasm of your staff in answering customers' questions.

- Appeal to shoppers' senses of smell and touch.

- Adjacent to shelving and racks that hold items to be purchased, have sample items that can be handled by the customer.

- Have staff frequently refold, repackage, and re-shelve in order to remove cues of product contamination.

- Provide hand sanitizer dispensers throughout your store.

- Stimulate browsing with interesting displays and with roomy aisles.

- Encourage people to bring friends and/or family when they shop with you.

- Hold special events at which you give how-to-use-it information and distribute free samples of reduced sizes of the product.

- When talking with a group of shoppers, repeat information in different ways to be sure everyone understands.

- Be ready to explain to a customer how the product or service will both protect from loss and allow for achievement of gains.

- Sell bare-bones versions of products and services with the opportunity for the customer to upgrade.

Make the Total Purchase Bigger

- Stock fun items throughout your store, each fun item close to more levelheaded items in the same product category.

- State prices not just as the total, but also as the cost per month over the expected useful life of the product.

- Merchandise larger sizes in order to sell more of the medium-size items.

8
Change Item & Brand Preferences

In retailing, we're often asking customers to make changes. It could be something that seems minor, such as encouraging the shopper to try out a new brand of a familiar product type. At the other extreme, the change might require the consumer to sign up for a completely different type of product or service, such as for the first use of an Internet-capable mobile phone or for home delivery of groceries.

There are all sorts of reasons you'd want to introduce a new brand or a new item to your shoppers. If it's a switch to your store's house brand, you are probably able to give the purchaser a better price and give your business a higher margin than with the nationally marketed brand. In addition, when the house brand products are produced to your private label specifications, you can maintain customer brand loyalty and advocacy even when needing to change the manufacturer or supplier behind the scenes.

With newly introduced items, you can offer your customers innovative solutions they can show off to their friends. The benefit to your business is that you may have negotiated a lower-than-usual purchase price from the suppliers because the suppliers want to build an initial following.

Some of the effective methods for changing item and brand preferences are similar to those I asked you to consider in prior chapters. For instance, pair the buyer's purchase with a demonstration of your—the seller's—social consciousness. Findings from University of South Florida indicate that pairing charitable contributions with the sale of brands unfamiliar to the customer will boost sales of those unfamiliar brands. The research finds that the boost is not nearly as great when it comes to brands *already familiar* to the shopper.

Now which of the many noble causes should you select? Ones which have a logical fit with the product category? Maybe a relatively strict logic, such as selling a newly introduced brand of kitchen countertop and contributing some sales dollars to Habitat for Humanity? Maybe a sardonic logic, such as selling an innovative development in exercise equipment and contributing some of the profits to an orthopedic hospital?

Surprisingly, those research findings from University of South Florida say the answer is that it doesn't seem to matter much whether there's any sort of logical connection between the product or service category and the cause supported by the contribution. What counts is that you select a cause important to your customers. Notice that this is different from what research finds to be true when a retailer's contribution to charity is used to head off consumer suspicions of price gouging. Then a logical connection is helpful. The example I gave you in Chapter 6 was of a retailer telling customers that the Red Cross would receive a portion of the raised price for batteries sold after floods damaged a community.

A few of the other methods for changing item and brand preferences could carry legal risk, depending on the jurisdictions in which you do business. For instance, many house brands are designed to look like the prototype product for that category. The prototype for laundry detergent in your market area might be Tide, so your supplier would make the house brand package labeling look like Tide's labeling. The prototype for mouthwash? If it's Listerine, you'd aim to have the house brand label look minty green or sky blue. For peanut butter, the prototype might be Skippy. Prototype electronics brands include Sony and Samsung. For beer, it could be Budweiser in a U.S. target market, but Heineken in the Netherlands.

CHANGE ITEM & BRAND PREFERENCES

The objective is to inform the consumer, not to risk violating the law—principally the Lanham Act in the U.S.—by confusing consumers into purchasing something other than what they want. Using the name of the prototype, sometimes you'll compare, sometimes you'll contrast, and sometimes you'll do both, but always with verifiable claims. "Tools that do the job like Black & Decker, but less expensive to purchase." "More all-round dental protection than Crest."

Selling an unfamiliar brand means creating in the shopper's mind a brand image strong enough to overcome the risks of purchase which always lurk when the shopper is making a purchase decision. As they look over this unfamiliar brand, they want to know, "Will this product solve the problem I'm buying it to solve or help me make the gain I'm looking for?" "Is it safe to use, both physically and socially?" "How much time would I need to invest in learning to make the best use of this product?" "What is this brand of the product really like?"

Answer the questions by hitchhiking onto the very strong images created by the prototype brands. These are the brand names most strongly associated with their respective product categories, and their manufacturers devote massive amounts of marketing support to maintaining top-of-mind awareness.

Findings from researchers at New York University remind us that with all unfamiliar items, the shopper has at least a little extra trouble navigating the maze that leads up to purchase. Help the shopper get there. In ads, signage, and face-to-face selling, work in phrases like, "...the same way as with the brand you're accustomed to using...," and "...once you do this a few times, it will be as second nature to you as what you've been doing up to now...." Just be sure you've reason to believe you're telling the truth to the shopper.

To accompany the new item, have easy-to-understand instructions. Don't worry if shoppers give the instructions only a glance. For one thing, there is research showing that knowing written instructions exist can be sufficiently reassuring for the customer. The purchasers don't need to read the instructions in order to feel comfortable. For another thing, the instructions ignored at the time of purchase are still important because we want to make it easy for the purchaser to learn how to use the product or service later, when they have questions.

Keep familiar elements in the format of the marketing and merchandising, too. Sure, when introducing a brand or product line, you can boost excitement by premiering a fresh look in your ads and in the layout of the store department. But unless you're launching a completely new business format, leave enough the same so that customers don't forget who you are.

Again, the shopper navigating the change to the new brand or item can be compared to a person navigating a maze. People complete mazes most quickly when there are signposts and benchmarks they can recognize and understand.

⁓

Some consumers are more venturesome than others when they consider entering the maze. Start by addressing your marketing and selling to those who welcome innovation and a bit of risk. Then, for whichever group you're working with, appeal to their distinctive purchase triggers.

- Venturesome innovators say, "I want the latest features, even if all the problems with the item haven't been worked out yet." Show venturesome innovator shoppers the most surprising things about the item. "Notice that the other end of the marker has an eraser."

- Respectable early adapters say, "I want a taste of where the world is heading." Explain to these shoppers the ways in which the item is an example of what the future holds. "This phone has room for expansion as new features become available."

- The deliberative early majority say, "I'll buy the item after it's proven to meet my needs reliably." Tell them about the good reputations of the item's designers and brand name. "You'll see lots of tractors like this used by the most experienced farmers."

- The skeptical late majority say, "Let lots of other people use it for a while before I buy." If you choose to make a marketing and sales effort with these shoppers, your best bet is to encourage them to try using the item with your offering to accept the item back for a refund or store credit if the purchaser doesn't like it. "Buy some of the brand you're using now and some of the new brand, and return for a refund any you don't use."

- Tradition-bound laggards avoid innovations and change. You probably won't be able to convince them to purchase the new, trendy version or maybe even switch to a different brand until the older versions are no longer being sold. Still, by listening to the objections of tradition-bound laggards, you might pick up some ideas for selling to the other groups.

With *all* shoppers, appeal to the prestige trigger. Many years ago, Iowa State University researchers decided to explore why certain farmers were purchasing innovative technologies while others did not in circumstances where the innovations were expensive when first made available. The answer to the why was that if the farmer could spare the funds, the fact that the innovation cost lots of money was actually attractive. It gave the farmer a head start and bragging rights that they had the latest and greatest before others could get it. Remember the story of Nikolai's tie.

RETAILER'S EDGE

The prestige appeal trigger sometimes works in indirect ways. Some cultural groups carefully avoid private label store branded merchandise in certain product categories because of prestige. Research findings from University of Memphis indicate that African-American consumers steer away from private label brands in clothing, particularly boys' clothing, because the private label lacks the cachet of widely advertised brands. Other research finds that Asian-Americans expect much more information about product features and consumer ratings when considering house brands than when considering national brands. To address these hesitations, advertise in media likely to be seen by people who are in your target market and are members of any cultural group that your experience tells you hesitates to buy private label brands in the advertised product category.

With all shoppers, you can help establish impressions of high quality for the new brand or item by listing the ways the private label alternative compares favorably to the nationally advertised prototype. "Buy our house brand because you get a larger package size for the same price." "Choose our new merchandise addition because it offers superior safety features."

- Make favorable comparisons between the private label and the name-branded items only if you've good evidence the comparisons are true.

- Don't overreach. An *Advertising Age* survey found that saying a Nissan Altima is as good as a Mercedes-Benz was more likely to earn an "Oh sure!" than an "Oh wow!" So if your private label brand is the Nissan Altima in its product category, better stay with comparisons to the name-branded equivalents to the Altima.

- Include tables and charts that make the differences easy to recognize. The shopper will be spending much less time looking at the ad or sign than you spent designing it. What you can figure out from looking at the comparison might be too complicated for the shopper who is in a hurry.

- Include a picture of the product you're recommending to the customer. If the product comes in a package, show the package, not the product itself. You're wanting to prime the shopper's brain to feel comfortable with the product package when they see it on the shelf. Familiarity—even recent familiarity—breeds comfort. This is especially important for the objective we're covering in this chapter, when what you're recommending is a product new to your shelves or is an unfamiliar brand.

- Do not show pictures of the products or product packages to which you're comparing the recommended item. Those other pictures would dilute the memory of the product package you're recommending. We want the shopper to keep the comparative advantages top-of-mind without picturing the competing products.

- And here's one you might find puzzling at first: In comparative ads, do not show pictures of people using the product. University of Maryland researchers discovered that such pictures lead shoppers to start thinking about using the products themselves, and when they do this, they put too much mental energy into thinking about just the recommended product. They forget to pay attention to the comparative advantages, so the special power of the comparative ad fades away.

Even when you're not making comparisons, using specific brand names with customers can be helpful. Is your shopper having trouble deciding whether to make a purchase? Present them with the names of some of the brands you believe would best meet both the shopper's needs and your store's profit objectives.

Researchers at University of Cincinnati and Miami University found that having brand names available to think about helps move indecisive shoppers forward in the direction of a purchase. Why does this work? Shoppers weigh the answers to two sorts of questions: The promotion-focused ask, "How would this purchase help me achieve a gain?" The prevention-focused ask, "How would this purchase help me avoid a loss?" By presenting brand names, the salesperson brings the decision from the abstract to the concrete. This helps the shopper figure out the answers and move on.

Don't suggest just any brands, though. Think through what provides the best fit for the prospective purchaser and for your store. When you give brand names, the shopper tends to focus the decision on those and eliminate other brands from consideration. This is especially true with your customers who are senior citizens. In fact, with elderly customers, it can be a disservice to mention brands that are a poor fit. If you name a brand and point out the faults, by a few days later, the elderly brain will too often remember the brand name, but forget that you said the brand has faults. If one of these customers makes a purchase based on that flawed memory and is irritated at the product's poor fit with their needs and wants, that can make your store and your salesperson look bad.

Be ready to answer questions about all brands your store carries. But in talking to the customer, accentuate the best-fit brand names.

༒

In Chapter 7, I described the ways in which appealing to the senses of smell and taste can help increase the total size of a sale. Those two senses plus others can also serve a role in changing customers' brand preferences or encouraging them to try a new product. With new products, talk to multiple senses. Gustatory sensations—the sense of taste—are highly relevant with food items.

There are two facts important to understand about taste: First, taste can be stimulated through associations from the other senses of smell, texture, sight, and even sound. Second, taste can be stimulated by verbal descriptions, not only by the sensory experiences themselves. And the more of these senses that are pleasantly stimulated, the more likely you are to move the shopper toward the purchase.

University of Michigan researchers presented one of two chewing gum ads to consumers. The first was designed to appeal to multiple senses, reading "Stimulate your senses." The other ad mentioned only taste, reading "Long-lasting flavor." All the study participants then sampled the gum. Those people exposed to the multiple-sensory version ad before the sampling gave higher ratings to the flavor of the gum. The researchers repeated the study using potato chips instead of gum and then with popcorn. In each case, the people receiving the multiple-sensory ad gave higher ratings to the flavor than did the people receiving the taste-only ad.

Having customers fully enjoy that first sample of a new product is crucial. When you include descriptions that appeal to the full range of sensations in your ads, promotional materials, signage, and packaging text or menu text, you gain the retailer's edge at the time the consumer puts your product into their mouth. And this method of achieving an advantage works even with non-food items. Whether it's detergent, sporting goods, or hardware, the fuller the preparation of the shopper's senses, the better.

Timing counts. Sometimes when people enter your store, they're on an item-specific mission. They know the precise product they want. They ran out of it at home and they need a refill *now*. Or they rush through the front doors of your shop holding the current ad or circular. Or they're fitting right in with the consumer psychologist's description of the adult male shopper, whose motto is, "Get 'er done."

But often, shoppers are coming in for a product, not for a particular brand or size. Here is your opportunity to guide their choices to what will both satisfy their needs and build your profitability. Whenever there are products you're featuring, you substantially increase the possibility of purchase by introducing those products to the customer very early in their visit.

Directly inside the store entrance, you could have a display of one package of each of the featured products. There's research that suggests you're best off showing these just to the left of the shopper as they come in. And you could have signs with brand names in large letters and very brief statements about product benefits. The research says this is best done on the right side of the customer who is entering.

The reason for these left-right differences has to do with how the brain processes information: Because shoppers usually walk into a store quickly without gazing around much, what the shopper sees often enters the brain at a subconscious level. Product shapes and brand name fonts perceived subconsciously will influence purchasing when they come in from the left side of the eyeballs. Brand names themselves and very brief product benefit claims are most effective when caught subconsciously from the right side of the eyeballs. You're aiming for small differences that, when put together, make big differences in profits. That's the retailer's edge.

You can magnify the effectiveness of these small differences by customizing them to your situation. I've told you where the research says to place the featured products. But watch your shoppers. As they enter your store, where do their eyes go to? That's gives you guidance about where to place a store directory, to position your staff member who welcomes the shopper to the store, and to display a preview of products you're featuring.

With the store guide and the greeter, do the placement directly where the shoppers look when they enter. Place any package display to the left of where the shoppers look, and place any features list to the right. Once you make your observations of shoppers entering your store, you might decide to reconfigure the entry area.

Different types of shoppers in different sorts of retail stores will have different habits. The single-mission shopper, who comes to a familiar sporting goods store for one very specific item, will promptly start looking for information about how to get to that item. The husband and wife walking into a furniture store with the intent of setting up a bedroom, dining room, and family room will be looking in a few directions. This is why you'll want to watch your particular shoppers and make store layout decisions based on your particular observations.

Among other things, you'll probably see that shoppers often pluck items from the rack or shelf without great deliberation. An observational study of laundry detergent purchases found that most people took no more than 8.5 seconds to select their item. With these low-involvement decisions, expect to make changes in purchasing habits only gradually. Suppose you want to build in the customer a habit for buying a house brand product. You might start out with a coupon good for a free sample of the house brand. If your recordkeeping system allows, offer this free sample at the cash/wrap only to those customers who purchase a competing brand in the same product category. This is for two reasons. First, research says that giving a free sample to people already buying the house brand decreases the value of the house brand in that shopper's mind. This is true even if the sample size is a special, smaller version of the regularly sold item. The second reason for giving the free sample only to those customers who already purchase a competing brand is that your prime audience for building the new purchase habit is among people already using the product category.

The next step could be a coupon for an item on which the house brand name is imprinted, with the item given when the shopper purchases the house brand product at full price. For example, the customer could get a free cloth shopping bag when they purchase two units of the product. Each time the customer takes their bag into your store, they'll be reminded of the pleasant experience in receiving a gift. Also, they and other shoppers seeing the bag will be reminded of the house brand.

In this example, the last step would be a few coupons that give what amounts to a twenty percent discount on the price. Research suggests that twenty percent is just high enough to motivate action. If the product quality is good enough, you've now started to build a new purchase habit.

Meeting the customer's expectations for product quality and customer service strengthens the trust that is invaluable when you subsequently ask those customers to consider changing to new brands or new items. Happy customers buy more. Researchers at University of Hong Kong and National University of Singapore found that joyful customers don't thoroughly evaluate all purchase alternatives. They tend to select either the first alternative or the last alternative suggested to them or that they come across.

〜

A retailing motto I've heard repeatedly over the years is "Always Exceed the Customer's Expectations." In my opinion, that motto is silly. Although fine-sounding, it doesn't work in practice. Every time you exceed expectations, it nudges the expectations up for the next time the customer visits. At some point, it is no longer profitable—or maybe even possible—to keep raising the bar for yourself.

In fact, the customer might not even notice if you *do* manage to exceed their expectations, unless the excess is dramatic. Researchers at University of Georgia and University of Southern California looked at situations where shoppers ended up feeling either somewhat better or somewhat worse about their experiences than they'd expected. When shoppers' expectations were exceeded, the shoppers often took it for granted and didn't give lots of credit to the product or service. It was when expectations were *not* met—when the store's promises were *not* kept—that there was more likely to be an impact on the evaluation of the product or service.

Rather than "Always Exceed the Customer's Expectations," I like "Regularly Dazzle the Customer." To ignite the positive excitement inside your shoppers' heads so they'll take your advice about considering new brands and items, all it might require is to keep your promises consistently. Do you promise the lowest prices in the area? The broadest selection? The latest distinctive merchandise? The quickest checkouts? That the new brand or new product you're suggesting will actually be better or as easy to use as the ones the purchaser is accustomed to? Whatever it is, be sure to have good reason to believe you can deliver.

༺༻

When we think of customer service, we naturally think about the one-to-one staff-to-shopper interaction. For instance, we want to be sure that every staff member is trained and coached to turn their attention to the shopper whenever a shopper approaches. But also keep in mind how powerful the signs and point-of-purchase displays in your store are in determining the quality of service you're providing.

Researchers at Columbia University found that an important element in signage is placing product choices into categories for the shopper. Categories help us break down the decision into more manageable steps. That soothes shoppers most dramatically when they're unfamiliar with the products they're selecting from. It speeds up decision making, and time *is* money for both you and your customers.

The power of categorizing is so great that even meaningless groupings made customers happier: The Columbia University researchers invited shoppers at a mall food court to select a free cup of coffee from a menu listing different blends. Consumers unfamiliar with the alternatives who selected from a menu listing the choices under headings Category A, Category B, and Category C were as satisfied as those who selected from the meaningful categories "Mild," "Nutty," and "Dark Roast." Both groups presented with the categories were happier than those presented with just an uncategorized list.

When you're requiring people to *pay* for the merchandise, they'll start asking, "What's the meaning of Categories A, B, and C?," so it's best that the division is designed to give useful information. As you walk the aisles of your store today, search for ways you might improve your signage to better serve your category-seeking shoppers.

Talking about categories brings me back to thinking about brand names, but this time from a different perspective: Each time you sell a product, you're selling not just the brand name of the item, but also the brand name of your store. So why should a customer buy that product brand name from you rather than from somebody else? One reason could be that you make it easier for the customer to distinguish products from each other based on what the products can do for the customer.

Don't confuse your shoppers with unnecessary technical specifications. Shoppers are more interested in what each of the products can do than in how the products do it. This point was put to use by computer chip maker Advanced Micro Devices (AMD). The company realized that consumers won't be buying an AMD computer. They'll buy a Dell or a Hewlett-Packard machine that contains an AMD chip. To distinguish themselves by making it easier on the shopper, AMD embarked on a marketing campaign in which the manufacturer can assign one of three labels to the computer: Vision Basic computers contain the AMD chip that has the best price/technology tradeoff for fundamental Internet use. Vision Premium computers hit the sweet spot for multimedia, and Vision Ultimate computers are for the heavy-duty video gamer. AMD talks about a Vision Black category for even more demanding computer processing.

AMD won't bother us with the technical details—that is, unless we want them. Then the details will be easily available. And according to researchers at University of Chicago and China's Shanghai Jiao Tong University, having the specifications clearly available does help make the sale, even if the shopper doesn't actually read the specs. In your retailing, be ready to fill in the technical details promptly whenever you realize the customer is looking for them. But make your lead story the different capabilities of the newly introduced brands and product choices you're offering the customer.

What we're aiming to do with all these techniques is to dislodge brand loyalty. If you get tuned into *when* a customer's brand loyalty is low, it opens opportunities for you to switch the customer to a brand which better fits their needs and better helps your bottom line.

There are what consumer psychology experts call "fortress brands." These are the ones which win deep allegiance from the consumer by becoming highly integrated into daily rituals, even quite mundane routines. Brushing my teeth doesn't feel right unless the taste of the paste and the look and feel of the tube are familiar. Still, this might be better thought of as "familiar habit" than as "brand loyalty." Operating on the other side is that variety seeking drive we all have to try alternatives. For some shoppers, the drive comes from wanting to lead a fashion. For some, it's a spirit of thrift plus curiosity to see if the house brand really is as good as the name brand. For all of us, it's the pioneering spirit we carry in our genes.

RETAILER'S EDGE

Venturing boldly where we have not gone before may seem better suited to Star Trek interstellar voyages than to a choice of toothpaste, but the basic principle is the same. Research by a team at Katholieke Universiteit in Leuven, Belgium, suggests that the itch to switch is strongest when the customer is hungry to fill a need. Your salespeople might be assuming that the customer who is most anxious to solve a problem is the one least flexible about considering different brands. But the truth is that customer hunger might be the perfect cue for the salesperson to explore alternative solutions with the customer. Coach your salespeople to pull this kind of highly ethical, highly valuable old switcheroo.

Encourage customers to make switches when they're moving from one role in life to another. This happens with events like college graduation, getting married or getting divorced, having a first child, changing careers, and settling into a new country or culture.

Again, we might assume that when people are already feeling uncertain about what's happening in their lives, they'd actually be less likely to switch brands. Since moving from one role in life to another is a time of uncertainty, it would seem that you trying to change brand commitments then would end up being a big waste. But when it comes to role switching, the truth is the opposite of what we might assume.

With this in mind, here are two tactics for you to build your profitability:

- Regardless of what products and services you sell, maintain easy-to-use gift registries where people due to graduate or to marry can list the items they'd like to receive from well-wishers. Hey, a number of Ace Hardware stores have wedding gift registries. Aside from the small appliances on there, I can only imagine how often duct tape appears. In setting up your gift registries, suggest items with brands that might be unfamiliar to customers, but which offer distinctive features for users and good profitability for you.

CHANGE ITEM & BRAND PREFERENCES

- Aim some advertising and store signage to people in your target markets who will be looking for evidence that they're doing okay in their new roles. Then think about brands which are or can be associated with status in those roles. Put these together so the ads and signage feature the brands in ways which convey the status benefits. Does it work? Research at University of Minnesota showed how recent immigrants seek out brands to give themselves acceptable status in their new culture. Research at University of Texas found that MBAs who are insecure about their job prospects are more likely than other MBAs to use products associated with successful businesspeople.

◦∽◦

Sometimes, sales staff can see a shopper narrowing down purchase alternatives too quickly. One problem with this occurs when the shopper ends up taking home or to their own business a product which doesn't fit their needs well or won't function well for them. The result is that they'll think less of your business, and you're not with them then to straighten things out.

The other problem comes up when the customer finds out there's a lack of fit to needs *before* they make the purchase. The alternatives get narrowed down, the customer concludes that none of the remaining alternatives will do the job for them, and they walk out without spending their money at your store.

You can go only so far in protecting customers from themselves. Along with this, your customer might truly know better than you what will fit their needs. It wouldn't come across at all well to the customer if you or one of your sales staff were to say, "Even if you tell me you want to purchase that specific item from us right now, I'll simply refuse to sell it to you."

Still, there are tactics you *can* use in this situation. Here are a few:

- Say it straight: "May I show you some alternatives that I think might help you select the best item for your needs?"

- Use the word "small." Researchers at University of Pennsylvania and Carnegie Mellon University find that with tightwads, you boost your chances about twenty percent by saying, "Here are a few alternatives that would cost a *small* amount more."

- Present *one* alternative which the customer considers to be a possibly better choice. Researchers at University of Southern California and University of North Carolina find that when a customer has shut down consideration of possibilities, doing this makes the customer significantly more willing to consider *a range* of alternatives again.

The balance between seeking change and reducing risk is exemplified so nicely by a question I came across on a "Yahoo! Answers" board. Next to a small picture which suggested to me the posting was done by a teenage girl, was this text:

"New unknown brands, similar to hollister etc.?

"My friends and I have been wearing superdry, hollister, jack wills and abercrombie for a long time but now they're pretty commercial, does anyone know of any upcoming brands of similar style? (we're not label whores in the slightest we just like the style and quality)"

Since I'm finishing up this chapter by using that example, and since teen fashion is not among my fortes, it's only fair that I also tell you what the initial reply read:

"heritage 1981. rheuls. mmm... roxy?"

Keep in mind though, that this "Yahoo! Answers" exchange occurred in November 2009. By the time you read this, the world is sure to have moved on.

RIMinders

- Target your marketing for brand and item changes to consumers who are likely to be going through life transitions, such as graduating, marrying, or blending into a foreign culture.

- In presenting new brands and items, appeal to the multiple senses of taste, smell, texture, sight, and sound.

- To highlight the advantages of the new item, compare and contrast it to items more familiar to the shopper.

- In comparative ads, include a picture of the product or product package you're recommending the shopper buy, but don't show people using the product.

- With shoppers who welcome change, talk about the new, surprising features. With shoppers who are cautious about change, talk about the good reputations of the item's designers and brand name.

- Use samples and coupons to introduce new brands and products, but don't give regular-sized packages for free.

- At the store entrance, display featured product packages off to the left and display very brief statements of product benefits off to the right.

RETAILER'S EDGE

- Categorize the choices for the customer.

- Advertise and publicize that you'll make a contribution to charity for each sale of a brand or item you'd like your customer to purchase.

- For new items, take special care to provide easy-to-understand instructions.

9

And You, Have You Given Enough Today?

It was in mid-1993 that development began on one of the most popular advertising campaigns ever devised. Jeff Manning, Executive Director of the California Milk Processor Board began work with Jeff Goodby, chief creative at ad agency Goodby, Silverstein & Partners.

The name of that campaign? "Got Milk?"

Here are some tips for retailer profitability inspired by the "Got Milk?" campaign.

- Start with current customers. Before expanding the target markets of the campaign, Mr. Manning and Mr. Goodby aimed to increase the amount of the white beverage that current milk drinkers consumed. Only after finding the success formula for doing this did they move the campaign to address the tougher sells, such as teenagers.

    In your store, I suggest you start with the retailer's edge techniques you feel are most likely to increase the profitability in your serving your current customers.

- Determine what your customers fear happening or what they yearn to have. Mr. Manning realized coming into it that milk itself aroused absolutely no passion. The product was plain white, and even the packaging was almost always perfectly boring. To sell more milk, he needed to fire up emotions. What he,

Mr. Goodby, and their colleagues discovered from survey and focus group research was that people felt terribly deprived even at the thought of having a brownie or cookie and no milk to drink with it. That became the passionate driver in the ads.

What are the emotional triggers for your customers and prospective customers? For those who are prevention-focused, what losses do they fear? For those who are promotion-focused, what gains are they yearning for?

- Keep the tone light and the content always focused on the core message. In the very first ad released in the "Got Milk?" campaign, a man ready to give a correct history trivia answer to win the prize on a call-in radio show can't get his mouth open because he's chewing a peanut butter sandwich when no milk is available. In a commercial used later in the campaign, the protagonist finds himself in Hell, where there are nonstop giant chocolate chip cookies along with endless milk cartons, but we see that every last one of the milk cartons is empty.

  Because you could be arousing strong emotions, such as fear and yearning, in aiming for the retailer's edge, find ways, such as humor, to keep a light tone in your advertising, signage, and personal selling. Otherwise, you'll put customers in a bad mood, and bad moods can depress sales. However, never allow your humorous touch to overwhelm your sales message to the customer.

- Work with partners, and think creatively about who your partners might be. The "Got Milk?" campaign co-branded ads with Oreo cookies. That was an obvious one. But then the CMPB arranged to have "Got Milk?" stickers put onto bananas, since a primary use for milk is in cereal, and people like to slice up bananas to put into their cereal. Mr. Manning partnered with convenience stores to have "Got Milk?" decals pasted onto the floors of the stores, with the labels directing the customers to the dairy cases. The CMPB licensed the slogan to dairy trade associations outside California for a fee. Realizing that the home base for milk is the refrigerator, they produced and promoted items likely to be used close by—items like baby bibs, aprons, dish towels, and oven mitts. All the items carried the "Got Milk?" slogan.

With whom might you partner to boost your business profitability, retailer? Think creatively.

- Keep the underlying message the same, but change the delivery to obtain the best welcome from those receiving the message. Mr. Manning and Mr. Goodby could not help but notice that in California, Latin Americans made up about one-third of the population, and this percentage was growing. Most were of Mexican descent. Mr. Goodby created a Spanish-language "Got Milk?" ad. But it turned out that the "Got Milk?" slogan translated into Spanish left many viewers of Mexican descent uncomfortable. They considered running out of milk as compelling evidence a homemaker had failed her family. The tag line was changed to "And you, have you given them enough milk today?"

In the chapters of this book, I've presented for your consideration a broad range and number of techniques to change the behavior of your customers. Now is the time to consider if you are changing your own behavior sufficiently. It will be a terrible waste if you do nothing different. So which of the techniques will you be putting into action starting today?

And you, how will you be giving your business enough of a retailer's edge *every* workday?

Acknowledgements

You'll notice that I've liberally sprinkled the text of the chapters with the names of academic institutions and other research sites, but I've not often told you the names of the researchers. I have two reasons for doing things this way. First, I want you to have sources to support the study findings. I thought you'd find it interesting to read location names you'd recognize, but might find it tedious to slog through names of people you've never heard of. Secondly, as I applied the research findings to retailing practice, I found myself drawing implications that sometimes did not strictly match what the researchers seemed to intend in their journal articles. I hesitate using the researcher's names because I don't want those individuals to be held responsible for my interpretations.

Still, I stay fully aware of how grateful I am to those consumer behavior researchers—and to the academic and other research organizations that host their work. I'm also grateful to the journals that published the articles. Most of the studies I've used as the bases for my conclusions were from peer-reviewed journals. This means that the findings stated by the researchers had to make it through a rigorous critique by journal editors who were themselves consumer behavior researchers. That makes for better quality control.

At the RIMtailing blog (www.rimtailing.blogspot.com), you'll find links to journals in which the research articles appeared. You'll also see links to blogs designed to serve retailers. I'm grateful to the moderators and the contributors on those blogs. The interchanges there helped me shape the consumer behavior research findings into specific tactics I could confidently recommend to you.

Lawrence Sander and Art Freedman gave me an abundance of ideas for improving the draft text. I took many of those suggestions, so I should share with them credit for the best parts of this book. At the same time, I blithely ignored the rest of their advice. Therefore, responsibility for the really terrible stuff here is mine alone.

And then there is a man I want to thank who did none of the research upon which my book is based, contributed none of the blog postings I recall seeing, and read none of the text. His name is Kemuel Anderson. He was my eleventh grade biology teacher at Anaheim High School.

Mr. Anderson firmly believed that in order to earn its keep, the study of science must have practical implications. When we studied botany in his class, the assignments culminated in designing a landscape plan for our home. The segment on genetics included a chromosome-based personal family tree, with attention to potential health problems. It is an approach to science which has served me well. When things started to feel a bit too esoteric during my graduate studies in psychology at Stanford University, I'd find relief in asking and then answering, "What difference does this make?"

My objective in writing this book has been to tell you—the retailer—the specific ways in which consumer psychology research findings can help you make a significant positive difference in your profitability.

Thank you, Mr. Anderson.

Index

Abercrombie & Fitch, 126
Accent lighting, 129
Accessories sales, 122
Ace Hardware, 30, 148
Add-on sales, 49
Advanced Micro Devices example, 146
Advertising, 27, 97
Advertising Age, 44, 101, 138
Advocates, 25
American Express, 72
Annals of Improbable Research, 87
Ariely, Dan, 87
Arizona State University, 22, 28, 93, 100, 127
Arm & Hammer Baking Soda, 19
Attitude change, 55, 133
Austin & San Antonio example, 71
Avon, 118
Ballpoint pen example, 86
Baruch College, 40, 70
Beckman Institute, 17
Benchley, Robert, 37
Best Buy, 12
Bilingual customers, 70

Birthdays & hometowns tactic, 61
Black Friday, 7
BOGOs, 5, 14
Brand loyalty, 133, 148
Branding, 29
British Airways, 126
Budweiser, 134
Build-A-Bear Workshops, 34
Burlington Coat Factory, 7
Burson, Katherine A., 45
California Milk Processor Board, 153
Camera selection story, 46
Carmon, Ziv, 87
Carnegie Mellon University, 21, 150
Case Western Reserve University, 45, 96
Cash/wrap, 66
Categorization tactic, 145
Cell phones, 24, 51, 85
Chain saw story, 57
Chain stores, 30
Changing attitudes. *See* Attitude change
Charitable contributions. *See* Contributing
Charlotte Russe, 118

Checkout areas, 67
Chewing gum story, 141
Children as consumers, 49
Church & Dwight Co., 19
Cif spray cleaner story, 84
Clark University, 89
Cleveland State University, 45
Clock story, 33
Coca-Cola Company, 95
Collectibles, 81
Color in retailing, 29, 72
Colorado State University, 35, 86
Columbia University, 48, 113, 119, 145
Comparative advertising, 138
Compulsive Shopping Disorder, 66
Conformity, 20
Consumption vocabulary, 46
Contributing, 49, 95, 133
Cooperative, 30
Counterfeit receipts, 11
Coupons, 6, 97, 144
Crowding, 7, 48
Crowning the Customer, 67
Cultural sensitivity, 39, 70, 118, 155
Customer dissatisfaction, 3, 96
Customer loyalty, 25, 38
Customer loyalty programs, 38
Customer referrals, 4
Customer relationship marketing, 26
Customer service, 14, 56
Customer values, 55
Customizing, 35
Damour, Jdimytai, 7
Database maintenance, 38
Defective products, 9
Digitas, 112
Duke University, 87, 122, 124
Dunkin' Donuts, 96
Ease of use, 105
Emigh Ace Hardware, 30
Emotions in selling, 60
Energy conservation, 101
Establishing trust, 28
Expertise dimension, 41
Extended service contracts, 21
Family shopping, 120
Fashion's Night Out, 119
Fast Company, 67
fcuk, 30
Femininity-masculinity, 23
Flam's, 21
Following up, 29
Foot-in-the-door tactic, 123
Forbes, 125
Fortress brands, 147
Fortune Magazine, 35
Franchisee, 30
Fraudulent returns, 11
Freedman, Art, 4, 68, 79
Frequent shopper programs, 39
Freud, Sigmund, 23
Frustration reduction, 98
Fun merchandise, 113
Georgetown University, 65
Georgia State University, 104
Gift registries, 148

INDEX

Goldman, Sylvan Nathan, 128
Golf putt story, 45
Goodby, Jeff, 153
Goodby, Silverstein & Partners, 153
Got Milk? advertising campaign, 153
Grandfather clock story, 33
Group shopping, 118
Habitat for Humanity, 134
Hard Rock Hotel, 125
Harvard Business Review, 25
Harvard Business School, 69, 122
HEC School of Management, 107
Heineken, 134
Home Depot, 82, 103
Hong Kong University of Science and Technology, 49
House brands, 29
Humor in selling, 64
IBM, 24
Ig Noble Prizes story, 87
IHL Group, 18
Indiana University, 6, 122
Indulgence products, 12
Information Resources, Inc., 84
Innovative consumers, 137
INSEAD, 61, 87
Inventory reductions, 19
Iowa State University, 41, 137
Jell-O, 19
Journal of Consumer Research, 43
Journal of the American Medical Association, 87
Jungian theory, 36, 43, 109, 114
Katholieke Universiteit, 148
Korea University Business School, 105
Lands' End, 35
Lanham Act, 135
Larger-package-sizes tactic, 124
Las Vegas Hilton, 126
Lasker, Albert, 106
Last-minute shoppers, 105
Life insurance sales tactics, 58
Lindstrom, Martin, 126
Listerine, 134
Loblaw Companies Limited, 67
London Business School, 122
Loyalty programs, 38
Macy's, 1, 36, 119
Making Money Is Not Illegal, Immoral or Fattening, 4, 68, 79
Manning, Jeff, 153
Manning, Kenneth C., 86
Mao Zedong, 83
Marks, Stephen, 30
Masculinity-femininity, 23
Massachusetts Institute of Technology, 87
McGill University, 3
Meat eaters story, 106
Memorial University of Newfoundland, 27
Meow Mix Wet Pouches, 119
Merchandise return story, 1

Merchandise returns, 1, 11, 36
Merchandise variety, 20
Miami University, 140
Mission shoppers, 115
Multiple uses of items, 20
National Retail Federation, 11
National University of Singapore, 144
Neiman Marcus, 93
New York Times, 44, 81, 119
New York University, 12, 113, 135
Newsweek, 44
Nobel Prizes, 87
Nokia, 24
Northeastern College of Business Administration, 63
Northwestern University, 24, 65, 79, 85, 114
Nostalgia appeal, 82
Novica, 118
Observation tactic, 143
Oklahoma State University, 104
Old habits, superstitions, and hand-me-downs, 3
Older employees, 17
Older shoppers, 140
Out-of-stocks, 18
Parity pricing, 79
Peacocks story, 25
Personalizing, 34
Philips Electronics, 123
Photography story, 46
Physical risk, 57
Possibilities shoppers, 115
Post-purchase reassurance, 28
Prestige tactic, 77, 137
Prevention-focused shoppers, 114, 124, 154
Price wars, 7
Price-quality link, 88
Pricing, 56, 78, 93
  discount pricing, 6, 22, 80, 87, 102, 144
  just-below pricing, 86
  price decreases, 95
  rounded-dollar pricing, 87
Pricing error, 12
Princeton University, 112
Prix fixe menu example, 79
Procter & Gamble, 93
Product instructions, 135
Product recalls, 9
Promotion-focused shoppers, 114, 124, 154
Quinn, Feargal, 67
Radboud University, 65
Recalled toys, 9
Red Cross, 95
Respect for customers, 69
Retail Council of Canada, 29
Return Fraud Survey, 11
Returns. *See* Merchandise returns
Rice University, 21
rimtailing.blogspot.com, 5, 78, 157
Risk reduction for consumers, 56, 61
Rituals, 73

INDEX

Russian tie story, 77, 81, 137
Saks Fifth Avenue, 82
Sales promotions, 6
Samples, 6, 120, 143
Samsung, 134
San Francisco State University, 40
Schwinn Sting-Ray, 82
Self-esteem, 51
Sensory tactics, 125, 141
Sesh, 118
Shanghai Jiao Tong University, 147
Shirt coupon story, 97
Shiv, Baba, 87
Shivashankar, Kavya, 71
Shopper conformity, 20
Shopping bags, 29
Shopping carts, 128
Shopping rituals, 73
ShopTogether, 118
Simplicity in products, 122
Skippy, 134
Smaller package sizes technique, 99
Social responsibility, 102
Social risk, 57
Sofa sale story, 104
Somers, Suzanne, 44
Sony, 96, 134
Sorbonne, 21
Space out items, 9, 80, 128
Special events, 119
Sports fan tactics, 117
Sprott, David E., 86
Stanford University, 13, 43, 71, 87, 110, 116
Star Trek TV show, 148
Stony Brook University, 6
Store advocacy, 25
Store entrance tactic, 142
Store name, 29
Store personality, 13
Superquinn, 67
Superstitions, 3, 10
Survivor TV show, 28
Teaming up, 29
Texas Tech University, 129
The Brick, 24
Three Musketeers story, 42
Tide, 134
Time, 7, 102
Time consumed, 34, 52, 80, 84
Touching-the-product tactic, 126
Toys"R"Us, 103
Trade-ins, 103
Trust, 28, 61
Tupperware, 118
Uncertainty advantage, 43
Unfamiliar brand selling, 133
Unilever, 84
Universidad Pública de Navarra, 62
University of Adelaide, 21
University of Alberta, 127
University of Amsterdam, 124
University of Arizona, 22, 93
University of British Columbia, 48, 61, 72, 113, 127
University of California, 6, 40, 126
University of Chicago, 112, 120, 147

University of Cincinnati, 140
University of Colorado, 119
University of Connecticut, 89
University of Georgia, 145
University of Hong Kong, 144
University of Illinois, 105
University of Iowa, 110
University of Kentucky, 73
University of Maryland, 21, 63, 139
University of Memphis, 138
University of Miami, 89, 104
University of Michigan, 3, 45, 55, 141
University of Minnesota, 50, 89, 149
University of North Carolina, 150
University of Oregon, 117
University of Pennsylvania, 22, 39, 40, 48, 93, 107, 113, 150
University of Singapore, 33
University of South Wales, 107
University of South Florida, 133, 134
University of Southern California, 6, 39, 40, 99, 145, 150
University of Texas, 98, 149
University of Toronto, 33, 120
University of Utah, 9, 110
University of Washington, 65
University of Wisconsin, 70, 73, 126
Values, 55
Variety seeking, 21, 148
Vasconcellos, John, 51
Verde Group, 29
Volkswagen Jetta ad story, 59
Waber, Rebecca L., 87
Wall Street Journal, 24, 49
Wal-Mart, 7, 86, 99, 111
Washington State University, 86
Web 2.0 tools, 44
Wharton School of Business, 29
Word of mouth, 27
Word processing software example, 105
Yale University, 63
Yelp, 97

Made in the USA
Charleston, SC
08 May 2010